MEANINGFUL
Work...

THE ENTREPRENEURIAL WAY

Your integrated guide to Career & Personal Life Management

I first met Judee shortly after I became the senior manager of a computer division in an organization where morale was very low and turnover was very high. In my search to 'turn the tide' in this organization, Judee helped me (a technical and task-oriented Information Technology executive) to much better understand and appreciate myself and the people who worked for me. Our group attended a series of personal development sessions facilitated by Judee and based on the concepts in this book.

These sessions helped my organization reduce an almost 50% annual turnover rate to only 5% and energized and motivated my staff and me to tackle the many issues that our organization faced. Under her guidance our collective morale rose dramatically and we made significant progress toward creating an enthusiastic and dynamic team. On a personal note, I know for certain that I learned from her and from the concepts and principles in this book a great deal about myself and my own career management efforts.

This book is an opportunity for you to "think out of the box". If you are not happy with the integration of your personal and work lives, read this book! Learning some of the concepts, principles and ideas in this book can have a tremendously positive impact on your life. Definitely meet "Ish" - I think you will like him. Judee's "Circle of Choice Dynamic" is a framework that will guide you through the many choices that you will face in creating a more balanced existence. We all want personal happiness and a sense of accomplishment with our lives. This book will give you lots of guidance!

Ken Clowes, PhD, C.A.
School of Business, University of Alberta

JUDEE REGAN'S

MEANINGFUL
Work...

THE ENTREPRENEURIAL WAY

Your integrated guide to Career & Personal Life Management

One's value system greatly influences one's ability to live a balanced existence. In *Meaningful Work...the Entrepreneurial Way* the reader is brought to an awareness of how values influence life choices and that changing or strengthening these values opens one to the possibility of a new way of living. Non-judgmental and compassionate, this book can be used for helping yourself or as a tool for helping others. Judee has made this a refreshingly clear read that does not require mental gymnastics to figure it out. The exercises address all learning styles...it is like finding under one roof, many of the kinds of tools I use in my practice. The reader can do one exercise or the whole book...either way it can be a life-changing experience.

Donna Foreman, RN,
Transitional Counselor

MEANINGFUL WORK...
The Entrepreneurial Way

Your integrated guide to Career and Personal Life Management

Available at all fine bookstores
World of Work Inc.
CALL TOLL-FREE: 1-888-839-4073
Fax: 1-204-985-9181
Email: hope@worldofwork.com
www.worldofwork.com

ISBN 0-9682037-3-6

PRINTED IN CANADA   [Cover design, book layout and design by iDeaMonsters - www.ideamonsters.com]

Introduction

For as long as I can remember, work, and in later years what I understood to be meaningful work, has held a great fascination for me.

I was five and a half in Grade One. When asked by a family member one day what kept me so long on the phone, I promptly replied that I was counseling my friend Billy. Later that same year, I was motivated by the cause of a school fundraiser and took top prize for the most sales in the school. A few years later when I was eleven, I talked the local druggist into creating a summer job for me at the gargantuan sum of $20 per week. When I reflect upon these stories…giving counsel, being inspired by a cause, and creating that which was meaningful to me…it affirms my belief that the seeds of meaning are laid down in our very early years.

My work education continued in university. There I learned, watching people who had done the same mindless work for thirty years, how truly meaningless work can be…an experience I shall never forget. When I graduated, I fought for and landed an amazing job. At the age of twenty, I had a company car, almost free rein to do what needed to be done, and very little day-to-day supervision. It was the first time that I truly knew what it meant to have my gifts used in a way that was meaningful to me. This experience greatly influenced the rest of my career…I have been my own boss for the last thirty-two years.

Much of the work I have done over this time has been meaningful because I saw work that needed to be done and convinced those in charge to hire me to do it. So I have a work history that has taken me many places. Over time I came to realize that all the while I had been observing how people "do" work. When I hear people say that they feel like indentured slaves or that what they would like most in their workplace is to be respected as a person and have their work valued, I wonder…what meaning can there be in 'doing' work this way? Perhaps the workplace systems that brought us to this time and place in our history were never meant to identify the individual's need for meaning. I believe that's something you have to do for yourself.

It goes without saying that the person who finds work meaningful and satisfying is happier, more productive, less stressed and more able to bring balance and joy into their career and personal life. I have written this book to share what I know about meaningful work and to show how to find it…the entrepreneurial way.

The birth of this book takes me to a place that is deeply rooted in my story…for am I not like the little girl who loved giving counsel, was motivated by a cause, and used her entrepreneurial skills for that which inspired and gave meaning to her life?

"The unexamined life is not worth living." SOCRATES

Acknowledgement

I would like to acknowledge the countless number of people whom I have worked with in the public, private and not for profit sectors over the last thirty years in my consulting practice. Collectively you have helped me understand the ever-changing face of the workplace and the challenges that individuals, regardless of title, are meeting on a day-to-day basis. These interactions have allowed me to put a human face to the workplace and those who work there…a most enlightening and inspiring experience.

In particular, I wish to thank the nearly 700 people, who over three and a half years, went through a work related transition program that I coordinated called Target U. Further, I wish to express my gratitude to the individuals who worked with me to deliver this program and who in this process helped model for the participants a meaningful work experience. The richness of the encounter grounded my knowledge and gave me very real insights into what works.

To those who supported my request for advice and constructive criticism in the writing of this book, I thank you. In my sincere attempt to truly hear what you were saying, I was taught new lessons in the arts of listening and discernment. This book is richer for your contribution.

I am deeply grateful to those kind souls who entrusted me with their story so that I might write their story. Although they have chosen to remain anonymous, they granted me permission to make use of my interpretation of their story where I believed it would make a difference…and I have.

My heartfelt thanks to my teacher, my associate and my friend Carol Ann Gotch, who contributed her knowledge and guidance in the creation of the Circle of Choice Dynamic, an integration of the principles of the Enneagram with my knowledge of the effort it takes to create meaningful work…the entrepreneurial way.

And lastly, to those who supported me in the personal drama I faced as this book unfolded…there are no words, just profound gratitude. From this experience I learned much about people, life and the power of the human spirit. I also learned that Life as The Great Teacher offers many gifts and unfathomable wisdom in our darkest hours. It is our job to find the meaning in such moments, for in that meaning is great energy, power and hope.

Ishmael is the wise one and he will be your guide. Ish says the difficult things that need to be said... the important things that need to be heard.

When you see this >

ISH has wisdom to share.

TABLE OF CONTENTS

4. Managing Myself..71

5. Managing My Perspective............................83

6. Managing My Development............................99

7. Hope is the promise of the future............149

NOTE: Many of the questions asked here in this book could require lengthy answers. You will find it helpful to have a notebook or binder for recording your answers and charting your Work-Life path and progress through the years.

🚶 Stories...

1

THE ENTREPRENEURIAL WAY

This book is based on certain universal truths that impact every aspect of your life. They are presented in this first chapter as the foundation upon which this book is written. Over and above these truths is a belief that to live life takes effort. Like anything...a sport, a musical instrument or an artistic skill, effort is required to do it well...so too with a life well lived.

Work comprises a good part of your waking hours and impacts heavily on the rest of your life. The concept of integrating career and personal life management is based on this very fact...that the two are inseparable. The better you can bring these two aspects into balance with one another, the more composed your life will be. *The Entrepreneurial Way* is about actively engaging in such a integrated Work-Life plan so that your work and your life can have more balance, more joy and more meaning.

Tools for the journey

...your gifts

These are the gifts that you the reader bring to the task at hand. They are the personal resources and character traits that are an integral part of the makeup of your person. They are the qualities that allow you to survive and thrive...the gifts of your ancestors. Some of these qualities may be well developed in you and perhaps others need work and with some guidance you can make use of your considerable gifts to facilitate your own integrated approach to career and personal life management.

...a dynamic mindset

Awareness: of your current reality...know where you are
Vision: have a dream...know where you want to be
Choice: move...without movement it is merely wishful thinking

...the Circle of Choice Dynamic process

This process gives you a career management path you can follow and allows for integration of the personal. You can always identify where you are on your path, and if for whatever reason you choose to leave for a time, there is always an entry point back.

...the stories

For each of the nine steps around The Circle of Choice Dynamic, there is an archetypal fable or fairy tale based on the story of a very real person. The people for whom these stories were written have no doubt faced many of the same challenges that you face in your life. These stories are powerful and hope-filled...and will enhance your process.

Spiral of continual growth and learning

One of the universal truths this book is based on is the Spiral of Continual Growth and Learning. This spiral shows us the whole picture of our lives. Our past, present and future are interconnected and they do affect each other. Looking at it in the larger view enables us to not only put our whole lives in perspective but also helps us be aware that there is a future, to create a vision for our future and to choose to work towards that future.

Our experience in the world around us tells us:

🚶 From a historical, technological and psychological perspective, the healthy pattern of life is growth.

🚶 Our personal experience tells us growth is a fact of life.

🚶 Our observation tells us that there are patterns to growth and a grasp of those patterns can facilitate the whole process!

> *Personal change, growth, development, identity formation - these tasks that once were thought to belong to childhood and adolescence alone now are recognized as part of adult life as well. Gone is the belief that adulthood is, or ought to be, a time of internal peace and comfort, that growing pains belong only to the young; gone the belief that these are marker events - a job, a mate, a child - through which we will pass into a life of relative ease.*
> LILLIAN BRESLOW RUBIN

Facilitate the growth process

- Acknowledge and accept your history
- Remember that failure to acknowledge your history can lead to repetition of past patterns
- Understand and believe that you can move out or beyond your history
- Keenly observe the present and apply appropriate skills to mold the future
- Sort through conditioning that you have received from parents, teachers, environment, friends, etc.
- Make some decisions about values that are important to you in the living out of your life and career
- Ultimately create a vision for yourself that leads to what's important to you

Path of growth

Here's what the sequence will look like when the path of growth is chosen.

COMFORT ZONES
Life seems to be moving well - we're comfortable with career, relationships, etc. This is a good time to get comfortable and set in our ways!

MOMENTOUS EVENTS
A crisis occurs. Either through choice or imposition, everything starts to change. This event can happen as a result of sickness, death, divorce, job loss, retirement, birthdays, moving out of the house, graduation, etc.

OBLIVION
We protect or insulate ourselves from pain by emotional withdrawal, numbness, confusion and/or immobilization. We don't know where to turn. We know that we have to let go of the past - it is over, but on another level, clinging to some kind of security, we hang on.

EXPLORING NEW HORIZONS
The next stage allows us to explore new solutions in our lives. This can take many forms: reading a book, discussions with friends or counselors, entering a program, etc. Make no mistake - it's not clear sailing - we are up and down in this stage. One moment things seem clear and another moment we are back to confusion and perhaps oblivion.

SEIZING THE MOMENT
In this stage you may feel drained - but you begin to say: "I've got to decide." There may be many questions like: for example "Is this right for me?" "Should I take the risk?" You take the risk and make the choices!

 ~ Stagnation is powerfully attractive but a precarious choice...
it can truly be a slippery slope ~

3

If you aren't growing you are stagnating

This is what stagnation looks like:
- Letting my actions and movement be dictated by external circumstances
- Blaming others, the company, for my personal fate...as if I have no personal responsibility in my own life
- Saying I have no choices
- Denying that the inevitable is going to happen
- Saying it won't happen to me

Your strategic approach

It is so important to take a strategic approach to career management and consciously integrate and balance your efforts with your personal life. Every aspect of this book is devoted to helping you do just that and the Circle of Choice Dynamic (which follows) guides your strategic process.

~ A healthy choice towards wholeness and well-being ~

SELL YOURSELF

Acknowledge your wisdom and recognize your transferable skills. Develop your self-confidence and self-esteem on an on-going basis...
you're worth it!

TAKE RESPONSIBILITY FOR YOURSELF

It is so easy to blame where you are on 'them' or 'that'. You do have the power to change things but you must start now to want it, to dream it, to make it your own!

CREATE MEANINGFUL WORK FOR YOURSELF

This process is all about you...about you taking charge...about you believing in yourself... about you creating career momentum!

Circle of Choice
DYNAMIC

Meaningful Action

Making a Difference

Clarity of Intent

Knowing Your Place

Priorities & Choices

Taking Responsibility

Vital Strategy

Interaction & Exchange

Obstacles & Commitment

What follows is a process that will guide you through the various stages of working your career management strategy. The four spaces on the right deal with that which is personal and meaningful to you and those on the left deal with you taking what is personal and meaningful to you to others. Meaningful Action is the place of change through choice. You can move around the Circle many times in your career...and like life, your movement at times may be unpredictable.

The Circle of Choice Dynamic process is comprised of:

1. the entrepreneurial traits you will need to rely upon to address what is asked for in that particular space
2. a short philosophical statement of what the space is about
3. links to various parts of the book that support what the space is about
4. Ask Ish wisdom to address some of the resistance you might be experiencing around what is called for in the particular space
5. Fables and Fairy Tales - stories of real people and their comments about their own story... a way to touch something deep within you and help you appreciate that you too have a story

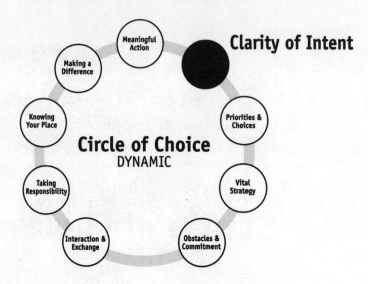

If you are not clear in your intention,
you will *never* really know why you are working.

The **Entrepreneurial Traits** that need to be *developed and expanded* here are:

SELF-DIRECTION
taking the lead and not waiting to be told

ENERGY
marshalling your resources so you physically move

FOCUS
getting down to what is really important

CLARITY OF INTENT

Philosophy

Work does not have to be a trial, although that is a popular view. Unfortunately it is not a view that offers much in the way of joy and hope. However, if you are searching for work that is other than a trial, work that is meaningful and makes you feel alive, you have to make the effort! Making that effort requires clarity of intent. You get a gut feeling; a stirring of your intuition and it is that which fuels your intent. When you have real intent you move. The vehicle to express your intent, power your movement and focus your effort is career management.

Career management is vital to:

- keep you on track…so you will be ready when opportunity knocks
- secure satisfying work…to help you be able to search out what would be satisfying and enjoyable to you
- open your receptivity to change…be aware of where you are going and know where change fits into your plan. In other words how do the changes 'out there' link to your intent?

Career management is necessary if you wish to acquire the resources to get what you intend. If your goal is to make your work life pleasurable and fulfilling, developing and working a career management strategy is a good way of reaching that goal.

Links

Intent is everything for intent is what you have in mind before it comes to reality.

To help you develop your career management strategy:

🚶 Read and do the exercises in *Managing My Future* as you will find it very valuable for casting light on a great many career and personal life issues. This is a good beginning for establishing intent.

🚶 *Managing My Approach* is very helpful for addressing issues of intent. The information on risk, urgency, motivation and commitment can help you establish if there is an attitudinal or behavioral issue that needs to be addressed.

🚶 *Managing Myself* offers excellent insights about finding the energy you will need to begin and to sustain a career management process.

Ish, I know you say we should have clarity of intent, but quite frankly, it really is a pain. I've come a long way without a career management plan. Why should I start now? Besides, all the people I know who have tried having one are no further ahead than I am.

It is very interesting when we experience our resistance to change or to starting over. We feel it is not fair that we should have to assess and reassess where we are and why we got here.

If you were on a trip and somehow or other ended up on the wrong road, you would know that if you continued on that road you would get somewhere - but that somewhere would not be where you had originally intended. No doubt in such a situation, you would go back to your map, retrace your steps and get back on the road you originally intended. And if you didn't have a map and weren't prepared to ask for help, then you would end up anywhere and you shouldn't be surprised if in the end that would make you unhappy, dissatisfied and angry.

And for those you see who are doing career management, maybe where they are is where they wanted to be at this time or maybe they should be going back to clarify their intent. Why not talk to them? Maybe you will find that these people who have a career plan are very comforted to have a map they can pull out when they get going down the wrong road.

Fables and Fairy Tales...
a story for every step of the way on The Circle of Choice Dynamic

The person for whom *A Hero's Quest* was written had this to say about their story.

"That someone else could see the hope... It helped me to see qualities in myself I might have forgotten. When I went deeper it was good to know they were there."

"Story is a tool for understanding what cannot be understood. At a time when details take over - it puts things in perspective. To see life as a range of peaks and valleys is more rewarding than seeing each pebble on a particular hill."

Your thoughts...

☗ *A Hero's Quest* ☗

Once upon a time, many years ago, in the land of Choice not Chance, there lived a delightful youngster, truly blessed with fine mind and pure heart. In the early years this young boy was a delight to all who knew him and it was easy for him to remember why he was here. He could bring light and warmth to the hearts of anyone. Even total strangers were drawn into his field of charm. Somewhere in the depths of his being, this old soul in human form knew that this gift of charm held great power…a power that when wisely used could change the unchangeable.

As a young lad, his imagination was sparked by Superman, a hero greater than life itself, who could not and would not be contained by the confines of a telephone booth…ever. He was born to fly, to use his power for right and justice, to in fact make possible the impossible. His sense of timing was masterful. And the world acknowledged his greatness…for his 'just in time' escapades that always saved the day.

But who can understand Superman? The world of Clark Kent hardly inspires, when he remains bounded by the four walls of a telephone booth. So the essence of this little boy's dream began to erode and became ever more distant. He started to forget why he was here. Sometimes he would remember but as the years went by…no one understood or cared to understand what the boy/man knew in the core of his being. He stood alone in a world that made no sense. Where was right? Where was justice? It did not exist and Superman was gone, long since forgotten, his power destroyed by men who forgot their boyhood heroes and lived in a world of cowardice and despair and sad women who settled for Clark Kent. The consensus of silence decreed that no one would come and save the day.

This caused great pain and agony for this young man. The pain and agony turned to anger. Don't they realize that I can make a difference? Why won't they listen? Will someone please listen…Superman is not dead. Please, he is not dead. And so he struck out on his hero's quest to find Superman and bring him back to Earth. How can we go on if there is no Superman? To be faster than a speeding bullet…and the young man became a speeding bullet, moving at kamikaze speed to feel as if he were feeling what he knew he should be able to feel if only the world could hear what he had to say. When he connected with others, which was rare, he was buoyed by their appreciation and enthusiasm for his ideas and his dreams, and he soared like a bird and felt like Superman.

And the hero's quest took him into the maze of worlds unknown and alien, the elixir of life for Superman, the refuse of a toxic wasteland for the questing hero. But take heart dear reader…Superman is not dead, nor is our questing hero. The impossible will be possible and that which is unchangeable will be changed. For the boy/man came to realize that the power was always within him to focus his eyes and bring the broken pieces together once more.

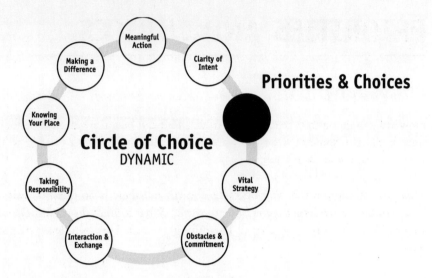

Priorities & Choices

As you pursue a career, you will want
to examine what is important to you

The **Entrepreneurial Traits** that need to be
developed and expanded here are:

INITIATIVE

building the 'head of steam' required to set priorities and make choices

---

DISCERNMENT

recognizing and accepting that you can't have it all and you can't do it all...that choices need to be
made and priorities must be set if you wish to experience Work-Life wholeness and well-being and
ultimately realize your dreams.

SELF-WORTH & SELF-CONFIDENCE

knowing that what you want is important

PRIORITIES AND CHOICES

Philosophy

How are you going to take care of yourself? This can be a time of great deliberation. Of course you want it all. But some of what you want is contradictory. (I want to be free to travel and I want to be seen as a real comer in my job.)

This process requires that you do make choices and there is no question this can cause a great deal of inner conflict. How long do you hope to work? What feelings do you experience around work? Are you angry? What are you angry about? How things are run? How people are treated? Are accomplishments recognized?

What do you want from the rest of your life? How much money do you need to retire? When should you retire? Will you be secure? Will you and your family be cared for? If you are clear on your intent, making these choices will be a little easier. But it is always a challenge.

You will have to learn to cut your losses...to think differently about the choices that have to be made. You can't have it all so what is it that is most important to you? This can be viewed as a painful process or an exciting adventure. Key to being able to set priorities and to make clear choices is a belief that you are worth the effort. Career management is your opportunity to learn new ways to take care of yourself and those you care about.

Links

There is a wonderful sense of humanity in this process! It hits people where they live!
You want to be sure that your family is taken care of and that they have what they need. Prioritizing and making appropriate choices requires evaluative judgments and clear decision-making. Some give and take is necessary. Make it an adventure, not a trial!

Managing My Perspective is designed to get underneath the difference between what you say and what you mean relative to attitudes about work. It can be quite an eye-opener to discover that your words could be covering up anger, anxiety or fear.

These reality benchmarks are interspersed throughout the workbook:
  · decide the fate of your own career
  · be proactive in your career management strategy
  · the world of work has changed...change with it
  · integrate your meaningful work intention into the reality of the world of work today
  · keep your eyes open to opportunities and possibilities
  · be flexible, adaptable and willing to learn continuously
  · try to deal with the here and the now...not how things used to be

Ish, you know I am so busy I hardly have time to get through my day. What with my job - very demanding, my children - very demanding, my partner - very demanding, the house - very demanding, I have no time. Someday when things settle down - but right now I can't be stretched another inch.

You know I can hear how frantic your life is...but be careful because by the time "someday" comes, your life will have been lived and you will have been the stagehand for everyone else's drama. And because you "settled" for that role, you never get the walk-on parts you would have treasured...forget about the lead role in your own drama.

If you say you have no choices - you have declared your intention. Setting time aside is quite simple. We always make time for what's most important to us. This space is about making your career management a priority. It is important to make choices of where you see yourself in the future so you are ready to meet opportunity when opportunity is ready to meet you. If you don't, you will get entrapped and sidetracked in doing everyone else's work and there never will be time.

The question here is, How can I best take care of my career management issues, so I can create Work-Life wholeness and well-being stability for me and mine?

Fables and Fairy Tales...
a story for every step of the way on the Circle of Choice Dynamic

The person for whom *The Golden Ball* was written had this to say about their story.

"I think philosophically it reinforces the thought that you need to take care of yourself first or you could become resentful looking after others. Do things because you want to, not because you feel guilty."

"It was like an acknowledgement that there was actually somebody looking deeper at what I'm really like - seeing past the surface. Not many do that - they see the top layer and don't go past the top."

"My friends don't see the real essence of who I am. This story caught that."

"It brought up things I never thought about... especially the whole concept of Driscule being the gift."

🏃 Your thoughts...

❧ *The Golden Ball* ❧

In a land of promise, in a field of dreams, there lived a child, a beautiful child, who was loved and cherished as no other, for this child was special, very special, sent as the one…the only one.

The child's name was Driscule. Fair of skin, dark of hair, she was a gift, a pearl of great price. She was everything one could hope for, she knew it, everyone knew it. The problem was that everyone forgot that she was the gift, and she somehow learned that she was to bring gifts, not to be the gift.

Now on her fifth birthday, our heroine Driscule was visited by her fairy godmother Edmar. Edmar had been watching Driscule's life from a distance and she was becoming very concerned. Something must be done to make sure that Driscule would remember why she was here. What could it be, what could make this child remember? Edmar had it. She knew what to give and she gave it. She presented Driscule with a ball of golden yarn, yarn to weave her dreams, to bring into the world her heart's desire.

But it seems the deed had already been done, the path laid, the course charted. Driscule somehow understood that she was made for 'doing' not for 'being' and being a good girl, she did her 'doing' in the light. It would only be in later years that she would understand that people of the light often must coexist with those who are no stranger to darkness.

And Driscule grew. She always took her ball of golden yarn with her, it was so very important to the person she would become. She used the yarn in many ways: to tie a bow on her finger so she would never forget - anything! To bind a wound; to tie around her waist, to keep all her tools close at hand so she could always do it right. She used the yarn to keep others out, to protect herself and to keep her emotions in, to protect herself. The yarn became for her the keeper of responsibility, guiding her and securing for her what she needed at any given time.

Dear one, each of us in our own way is given a ball of golden yarn to weave the intricate mosaic of a conscious life deeply lived. Oh, it might get frayed or even unraveled but if we always hold on to a thread we will never lose our way.

Driscule's fairy godmother Edmar gave her the golden ball of yarn to remember the essence of who she was and why she was here. Driscule learned well to use it to the benefit of others, but when will it be her turn? Is she now ready to use it for her own deliverance?

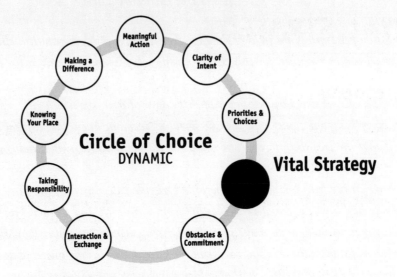

Vital Strategy is a combination of
dreaming, vision and hope
and the 'know-how' to get it done.

The **Entrepreneurial Traits** that need to be *developed and expanded* here are:

WORK ETHIC
there is value in just putting one step in front of the other

---

SELF-KNOWLEDGE
be clear on who and what is driving your life and your commitments

---

VISION
the ability to know your dream and let it power you into the future

---

VITAL STRATEGY

Philosophy

The very human part of you often ends up taking care of the dreams of others and you have no idea what your own dream for yourself is about. You live in a society that more often than not would say that dreaming is a waste of time.

But consider sports, in particular the Olympics. You see the young athletes when they are interviewed. Invariably they say "I had a dream" and you can feel the power that that dream held for them. It fuelled them through the tough times. Even if they miss the gold, just being there is a spectacular accomplishment for them. For most of us it would be true that if you have a long held dream you have within you the gifts and talents, whether developed of dormant, to bring your dream to life…if you are willing to put in the effort.

A critical part of the career management "game" is having a dream. Dreams serve as an energy source to support and buoy you on a bad day and fuel you into the future. Many dreams don't surface until you are older. It seems you need to live life to help give your dreams form. As you get closer to your dreams, they may change, but the core of the dream remains.

Links

This can be very exciting!

- If you take a time line into the past and retrace your steps, often you can see the path in your dream continuum that has brought you to the present moment.

- *Managing My Future* touches what is important to you in your view of the future, which of course touches on your dreams for the future.

- Some skeptics have difficulty believing that dreams have any value whatsoever and they stopped believing in dreams long ago. The fact is that dreams give us energy from the future and *Managing Myself* has a very good exercise that you will enjoy.

- *Managing Myself* speaks of holding on to past hurts and how doing so depletes your energy supply for living in the present. It is difficult to have the vital energy to do what needs to be done if you are living in the past. A good exercise accompanies this discussion.

Ish, it seems a little ridiculous. I am too old to dream! I learned a long time ago that dreams might be fine for others, but me, I'm just surviving. If you had any idea what I do in a day - you'd realize how ludicrous it is to even think that I can handle more.

Well, when you say that, there is one thing that immediately comes to mind. It is obvious to me that it is easier for you to say "no" to what could make your life richer, happier and more meaningful, than it is to say 'no' to all those demands, obligations, "shoulds" and "oughts" that the world seemingly requires of you.

No one is going to force you to do career management and no one can force you to dream. But I will tell you - when you were young you had dreams. What was it you dreamed about? Dreams energize and help give us a sense of direction. Your dreams are important...and if you will take the time and take the risk to discover what you long for, you can begin to make plans to get there.

Career management is a lifelong process. Dreams unfold and your life will also unfold...for that is what lives do. With your dreams overseeing your life process, you will find life more meaningful because you will be engaged and more fully alive.

Fables and Fairy Tales...
a story for every step of the way on The Circle of Choice Dynamic

The person for whom *The Quality Connoisseur* was written had this to say about their story.

"I can't think of anybody I would talk to except you."

                "Yes, it said you cared. No one really cared (about my story)."

"I know it (my story) is there - I won't hang it up someone
might see - it could hurt negotiations - there is no place for
me at home to put it."

                "No, the story was nothing new. I focus more on every-
                one and everything rather than myself."

⚚ Your thoughts...

♞ *The Quality Connoisseur* ♞

As I sit and reflect, I remember a man much younger than me who knew what he knew and he knew it very well indeed. One day this man decided to strike out and seek his fortune.

For years he had put in such long hours and traveled so much. It became hard on him and difficult for his family. When he looks back he feels he missed a lot of his children's growing years. In business, it would frustrate him that sometimes his clients would listen and sometimes they would not. They were too busy or too locked in to their own way of thinking to be able to hear that there was another way. What bothered him the most was that if there were snags or problems, these clients wanted to blame the problem on him. He hated being blamed for something that was not his fault. To blame someone who tried so hard to deliver a quality product seemed so unfair and so disrespectful.

And so he decided to start his own business. This would allow him to be with his family more often and to do things the right way…the way he knew a business could be run.

He knew what to do and what not to do. He was committed to doing things differently and doing them well. He was going to run his business efficiently and make his company the very best place to work. Quality was his guiding principle. He understood that quality meant more than machine parts working smoothly together and that quality was about timing, balance and harmony. To make a beautiful, quality product required care and attention to detail and he wanted to hire talented people who would make his dream come true. He knew he could make these people care as much about his dream as he did.

He vowed when he began that his company would be the best place to work and it was. Over the years, he tried in so many ways to show his care and concern for his employees…in sickness and in health. He was an honest man who believed that his word was his bond and he made it a policy to offer quality money for quality work. And the business grew and grew rapidly and as the business expanded, it became harder to be the kind of leader, husband and father he wanted to be. The price of success meant long hours of work and far fewer hours at home than he had anticipated when he chose to start this business. The price was far higher than he had imagined.

And with the rapid expansion, things changed. Staying close to his people became more difficult. He was trying so hard to keep his promise and make this a good place to work but the more he tried it seemed to him that everyone expected so much more from him. Everyone was quick to blame him if things weren't just perfect. He hated when people blamed instead of trying to help to make it better. Did no one ever think to say thank you?

And when you think of it…wasn't this where this story began?

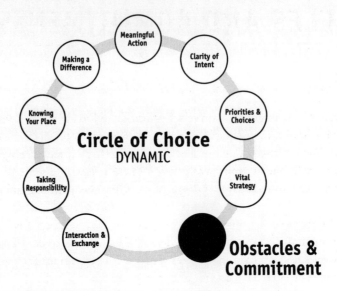

You start to wonder why you
started this in the first place.

The **Entrepreneurial Traits** that need to be
developed and expanded here are:

INVENTIVENESS AND RESOURCEFULNESS
seeing 'outside the box' on your own behalf

COURAGE
the pluck to move forward in the face of risk and no guarantees

TENACITY
the ability to keep truckin' long after the rest have given up

MOTIVATION AND COMMITMENT
the strength and determination to champion your own cause

OBSTACLES AND COMMITMENTS

Philosophy

You have discovered your intention, you've set priorities and made choices, you have developed a strategy and now...you have a momentary letdown. "It is going to be so much work; it isn't turning out exactly the way I thought it would...poor me! I tried following a career management process once before and it didn't work then and it won't work now!" There is clearly a sense of hopelessness. This is the moment when you have to rediscover your purpose. What was your original intention?

Once you have experienced the obstacles, have reassessed why you began this process in the first place, there comes a moment of commitment. You decide you are going to do this no matter what. So experiencing the obstacles and overcoming the resistance are a very important part of this process. Having overcome resistance you now have a sense of commitment.

Links

Realign your energy!

🏃 It is easy for you to settle into this place of feeling that you have been dealt a bad hand. We all have lived in this place many times in our lives. You can put a lot of your effort into maintaining these feelings. This is the place where there is a lot of blaming and "if only". These thoughts are often directed to others.

🏃 It is all energy that is expended for no useful purpose. It does nothing for you and it gets you nowhere. It is in fact a waste of energy, and energy is the very important commodity you need to fuel your career management process.

🏃 The later pages of *Managing My Approach* deal with motivation, commitment and momentum...very important entrepreneurial traits you will want to tap into. When you are addressing your obstacles, *Managing My Approach* also addresses many of the negatives you might be experiencing and invites you to turn those negatives into positives.

🏃 It is important to understand that they are worth the effort to get yourself out of this place. Just getting up and doing something is a good place to begin. Battling the feelings of inertia you experience at this place is a challenge. Know that it is important to move; otherwise you will get stuck and could stay at this spot indefinitely.

Ish, I've tried - there is no question I've tried. I followed the steps: clarity of intent, priorities and choices and I spent a lot of time coming up with what I considered a vital strategy. And not one thing is working. The boss piles on work daily and my partner seems to be working full-time to give me a hard time and I didn't get into the course I applied for.

You are obviously having a difficult time and it is at this point on the Circle where we feel we want to throw in the towel. "Poor me - it's not fair - everyone is conspiring against me." It is not a nice feeling.

This is your opportunity for renewal. Know that few things in life are straight and smooth and know also that no one is going to force you to undertake career management activities. And these people and situations you are angry about - well, they aren't going to make your future happen - you are. So it boils down to this...there are obstacles and no doubt there will be more along the way but that form of resistance calls you to make a renewed commitment to your process. Go back and re-clarify your intent and move forward with renewed commitment. And know that it is hard to do this work on your own, so be sure and find a mentor who will cheer you on, nurture your dream and above all - will tell you the tough stuff when it needs to be told.

 # Fables and Fairy Tales...
a story for every step of the way on The Circle of Choice Dynamic

The person for whom *The Energy Machine* was written had this to say about their story.

"It made me take a right turn in my life...I am now being fed by nature - I am discovering myself. Taking a different approach at work...it's not my life."

"Seeing your life on paper can be an eye-opener. Self-knowledge, self-understanding ...it was important to have someone listen to me. I'm a private person - it was hard to see what you heard (me say)...it bypassed my defense mechanisms."

"I keep it in my office. My family didn't see me in the story, they laughed at me. My brother didn't recognize me in it...made me realize that there are other things in life other than work. I'm seeing life differently."

🏃 Your thoughts...

✳ *The Energy Machine* ✳

There once was a dear little child, delicate of nature, and who like most everyone else, deeply desired love and attention. As a young girl, she danced ballet and played the flute. There were those who thought her very promising. But she herself never thought she did very well...yet that was just her opinion, for at her core, she believed if she could not be the best, then the rest was not good enough. As she grew into adult life, that belief would be a mainstay of the person she came to be.

In school only the most creative of teachers would have been able to appreciate her particular interests in learning. Science to her was enthralling, if she was drawing the laboratory apparatus, and geography was exciting, if she could sketch the maps. It was this passion for the artistic that ultimately ushered her into the world of fine arts that she was to love so very much. It was a virtual smorgasbord of artistic treats that truly fed her soul. In all of this she learned that in her mind's eye, she could see in 3D, a unique gift given to a very few. She could design an object and know what the back would look like even though the back was not visible. Does this suggest perhaps a special gift for seeing what others cannot? Her world was a world of form, design and color. Her life at this time was the life of a vibrant, vivacious woman who though shy, relished her friendships, her parties and her life.

And then it was time to wake up and smell the roses...to make it in the real world. We all know that art is fine, but it doesn't put food on the table...or so 'they' say. So she went to work. Work was something she knew about. For her, work is excitement, a seeing of what's been accomplished...a work in progress perhaps, a sense of pride. And always work was bounded by an insatiable desire to please others.

And the years go on. Being very bright and looking to her future, she finds herself in an opportunity where her creativity is constantly challenged; for daily she finds herself making a million decisions. As she scurries through her work, she fashions order and efficiency in a factory with the finesse and craft of the artist. She is like a well-oiled machine, a machine that fairly flies through jam-packed days, days filled with challenges and children choices, duties and exhaustion, school lessons and worries and always loneliness and wonderings.

She is an energy machine. Work gives her a purpose, a reason to get up in the morning. What would she do if she could not work? She is shy and isolated and has few friends, for in these times ...how does one know whom to trust? Work is her lifeline, yet one wonders, what fuels the Energy Machine?

There is ancient wisdom which asks...dear one, when did you stop dancing, when did you stop singing, when did you stop telling your story? This little story that you have told today tells clearly of your passion. It is a beginning, a remembrance of your heart's desire, which always was and will remain your energy source.

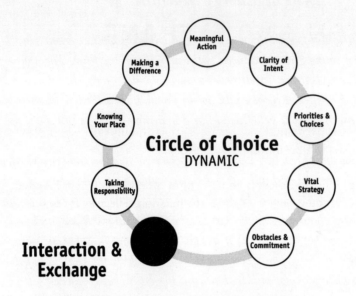

Circle of Choice
DYNAMIC

Interaction & Exchange

Here there is a sense of renewed life...
starting again.

The **Entrepreneurial Traits** that need to be
developed and expanded here are:

TIMING
that moment when it is exactly the right moment to make your move

REFOCUS
although conditions may occasion minor changes, keep your attention on what is meaningful to
you, realign your intent...don't get sidetracked

SELF-CONFIDENCE AND SELF-WORTH
a belief in yourself and your ideas

INTERACTION AND EXCHANGE

Philosophy

This is the place of transition. We move away from the personal soul-searching of the first four steps to the more impersonal. Where do I fit into the bigger picture?

If you are seeking meaningful work, there is an element of stewardship that is involved. "Here are my goods and services, where can they be best used?" is the question. The answer rests in the word "meaningful". You are going beyond yourself to find work that is more than just a job. From a career management perspective, it means starting a path for you. Where do you want to end up? Where do you see yourself fitting in? It is time to not only gather information but to use it.

The temptation at this step is to fall into over-researching. There comes a point when acquiring more knowledge can be an effective method of dragging your feet, an excellent avoidance tactic, a way of hiding. It is understandable and no doubt at the root is fear…fear of change, fear of trying something new, fear of realizing your dream.

You are looking for a connection, something to energize you. This means that you will have to declare yourself and your intention. It means future forecasting today where you can best fit in and make a contribution in the future

Links

This step of the process requires taking risks and being a strategist.

🚶 It requires that you stop being secretive about what you would like to do. For example, if your company is involved in a merger, this is the time you would be actively examining options for your future in the new company that will be formed. From your perspective there is a risk. You are concerned that by declaring yourself something might happen to you.

🚶 In reality your wisest step would be to explore how you feel you could fit into the expanded new company that will be formed. Don't wait for your company to guess where you fit in…give them options. As you explore your options, other possibilities are sure to present themselves. Keep your ears, eyes and mind open and then use your knowledge to further what's important for you.

🚶 Choose a growth and development task from your Personal Development Action Plan at the conclusion of *Managing My Development*. Decide how you are going to make this happen. Be specific.

This step plain and simply scares me to death. Every time I think of letting my intentions be known, all the awful things that could happen come flooding in. I must not be ready. I think I should think this through again...for what seems to me the hundredth time.

Well, you know you're in the right place if you are having those feelings. It is challenging to take the risk and put your ideas out there, and declare your intentions. I ask you though - what is your alternative if you don't take the risk?

Putting your ideas out there is a conscious exercise that needs to come from a hope-filled place. You are not sure what the exact outcome will be and you have no specific expectations...but you are hopeful. Know what you want to say and how you want to say it and remember, the most effective way to engage someone is to show him or her how your solution meets their needs. That approach eliminates 'why I want you to do this for me'.

Remember, you are offering goods and services. Those you talk to can more easily hear what you are saying if it is not about you personally. It creates space for them to view your proposal from a broader perspective.

 # Fables and Fairy Tales...
a story for every step of the way on The Circle of Choice Dynamic

The person for whom *The Weaver's Dream Carpet* was written had this to say about their story.

"I think the whole notion is neat. It is not private - it's out there...a story."

"It is about expression. What is the catalyst for any form of expression? It is an invitation to wake up..."

"People want to help themselves. It's a fun way of helping yourself get out of your snag...See (your) patterns".

"The story says I'm worth it."

"Hitting me over the head with what I already knew. Certain things still matter."

"The Carpet's threads being refurbished. Hopeful, life-affirming. The notion of yearning, the threads being fixed."

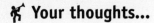 **Your thoughts...**

☊ The Weaver's Dream Carpet ☊

Very long ago, in a land far, far away, there lived a gifted weaver named Cholm. He would sit at his loom day after day and weave the finest of tapestries and carpets. People came from far and wide to watch his hands fairly fly, as he created one masterpiece after another. To the world, Cholm was the happiest person in the land.

But in his heart, Cholm was a very unhappy man indeed. For it seemed to him that every day he was forced to go to his loom and work from dawn to dusk and as time went on, every carpet seemed the same as the last. He had no sense of freedom - he felt like a cripple, chained to his loom.

One night Cholm had a most intriguing dream. In the dream he was weaving an exquisite carpet - but this carpet was very different from any carpet he had ever woven thus far. It was as if this carpet was dancing, like it couldn't wait to be released from the constraints of the loom. Cholm awakened from his dream and decided right then and there to create such a carpet. This carpet would be able to go where he could not and then come back and tell him stories of adventures he would never have and describe far-off lands he would never see.

As he crafted this carpet, he thought, with every graceful movement, of his lust for adventure, his craving for the reckless, his joy and love for a life he would not have and the person he could not be. All of this and much more were woven into the fabric of his amazing Dream Carpet. As he wove, the Dream Carpet began to dance…it was taking on a life of its own…it wanted to MOVE! He called his Dream Carpet Saitai…that in his language meant 'my precious'. As he released her from the loom, he asked her to promise to remember from whence she came and to always come back and tell of her adventures. "I will be your safe place and will always take care of you."

In the beginning Saitai kept her promise to Cholm. She would go to strange lands - but she kept her secret of who she was under wraps. Only she and Cholm knew she was a carpet like no other. But as time went by she remembered Cholm less and less. She would come back to have her threads refurbished and she would reluctantly tell Cholm of her adventures. There was so little time and so many adventures to be had. She was young. Why waste her time…especially on an old weaver?

And the years went by. Cholm was once again brokenhearted. He realized that instead of living his own life, he had tried to live his life through another - his beloved Saitai. He knew in that moment that he could no more be a carpet than a carpet could be his dream. Saitai, who could never remember anything but her dream life, was also having misgivings. She longed for her life of adventure, but was more than a little aware that parts of her were becoming threadbare. What if she were no longer beautiful? What if she could no longer fly?

But all is not lost…it rarely is. If Cholm could find a way to live his dream and Saitai could dream new life into her fantasy world…working together they could find happiness and freedom, knowing that the most important thing they had to do, as they moved into their future, was to care for each other.

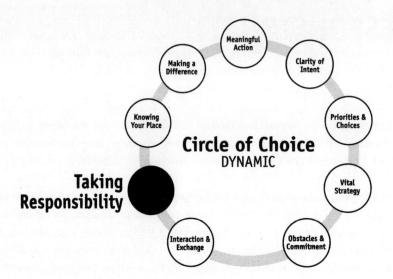

It is about learning to trust your gut instincts
and to be vigilant on your own behalf.

The **Entrepreneurial Traits** that need to be
developed and expanded here are:

_____

TIME MANAGEMENT
being able and willing to make time for today's obligations and tomorrow's dreams

_____

DEDICATION AND TENACITY
a willingness to chart your course and the courage to stay the course

_____

DISCERNMENT
reading the signals and choosing what needs attention

_____

TAKING RESPONSIBILITY

Philosophy

This is a very challenging phase in the process because it asks you to accept that you do have choices. It asks you to tap into your inner knowing that tells you what's important for you. In other words, no one knows better than you what you really want and no one other than you is going to get it for you!

Many times you get stopped in your track right here. I can't change, "what about..." and the list of people you owe is endless. Often we are so busy doing what other people expect of us, we never stop and ask ourselves, "But what about my loyalty to myself?" Examine your feelings about your loyalty to your employer. You have agreed, in your formal or informal contract, to what your work arrangements with your employer will be. Just always be aware that there is a big difference between loyalty and indebtedness.

Career management in this space involves being split between where you are and where you choose to be. It also addresses the issue that you are busy, that you have a job. How are you supposed to manage your career at the same time?

This phase of the Dynamic is about managing your time and space. It is important to just keep putting one foot in front of the other and manage your daily affairs. Try not to become too confined in your focus nor conversely to become too scattered and..."don't jump if you're not sure."

Links

Managing My Perspective is another piece of the "where do I fit in" puzzle and deals with specific aspects of what you think about your current position. It ultimately challenges you to try to find out if what you say is really what you mean.

The Meaningful Work Indicators Assessment addresses those aspects of work that have particular meaning to you. Knowing what is important for you could be of great benefit in helping you figure out just exactly what path to pursue...where you fit in.

Managing My Development reviews seven key areas of generic skill development and helps you understand what you are really good at and where you need to do some additional skill building. In a career management process, this information is very important.

Ish, I know this is about me making choices, but I'll tell you it doesn't feel that way. I have feelings about what I'd like to do but I've worked for this company for eighteen years. They've been good to me and my partner thinks I'm crazy wanting to strike out on my own. I feel indebted to the company and so unsupported by my partner and very, very guilty. How can my gut reactions be telling me one thing and my world telling me another?

Well, the fact is it can. This space of Taking Responsibility can be most challenging because things like loyalty and indebtedness do get confused, and not immediately getting from those we love what we want and need, can be crushing. As you live with this and work through it, you might want to consider the role of irritation in the formation of a pearl of great price.

It is important here to have both feet firmly planted on the ground. Retrace your steps around the Circle and review what got you here. If you feel your thoughts are congruent with the career management work you have done thus far, I'd say you are in the right place. And remember, this place requires that you "trust in the process". You have work to do while you are dealing with this phase. Understanding and trusting what you really want takes work and it can take time. These things don't usually materialize overnight.

And finally be prepared to forgive yourself for what you are unable to give on a given day and forgive others the same. And be patient...it will unfold.

 # Fables and Fairy Tales...
a story for every step of the way on The Circle of Choice Dynamic

The person for whom *Laughing Tears* was written had this to say about their story.

"The story helped me put me in perspective. This story has allowed me to see the value of choosing a path and then taking it."

"Insights, understanding, reaffirmation, clarity, move out of the tragedy and denial of your life - forgiveness".

"Someone cared enough to listen. I was amazed at what you saw from what I told you. You put an emotional framework around facts. It shows I am a unique person with unique particulars. It allows another to see me as a person."

"I was surprised my story was a story."

"I am more conscious of who I am now relative to the past."

"You made leaps - you saw more good in me."

✸ *Laughing Tears* ✸

Gather round, dear children, for this is a very strange tale indeed but one that is nonetheless true... that one day long ago a very special clown was born. This clown whose name was Philo, was one of the few clowns ever born who arrived in this world AS a clown. In the beginning Philo remembered this but could not speak his truth and in the end, he plain and simply forgot.

As his birthright Philo secured a bit part in a traveling road show. He really loved that life although in the beginning, he was only part of the chorus. He felt secure there...he felt he belonged. He relished this feeling of his person being deeply rooted, for in some part of him he understood that to build anything, you must begin with a solid foundation. But a traveling road show must keep moving and a child inevitably grows and so it was with Philo. He donned his red nose, for his clown training had begun in earnest.

*It was as if he had been catapulted from a nest of loving rootedness into a whirling dervish world of unkindness and derision. He learned he was stupid, only to learn in later years that he was brilliant. Although 'they say' the last shall be first it seemed from his vantage point the first was merely last. He learned that not trying worked and although it afforded him entrance into the world of misfits in truth, in his heart he was a warrior and he never gave up. And he grew into manhood.
His rootless life had left him as a man without a country and thus he sought citizenship in love. He would learn only later that coming home is an inward journey and loving yourself is at least as important as loving others. With all this sadness, he was beginning to understand why the clown's nose is always red.*

He became a star - the clown's clown. Well, what does one do when one reaches the pinnacle and one has not left this world and is in fact still very much alive? Apparently one goes back to school...for it would seem the school of life had much more to teach our young Philo.

And so he learned that stars must be part of the herd - does he know they still shine? And that security must be secured by no longer taking risks - does he know that each can live with the other? And that the unclear vision of his future has clarity because he cares and the pride that he finds in his work is the antidote to the meaninglessness that most others feel. Perhaps the greatest gift our Philo learned along the way was how to build...how to manifest the unmanifested, step-by-step.

And you might ask why this story? Why not a story of circuses and big tops, tents and lion and tigers and bears? Well, perhaps if we read between the lines, it is all of that and more. To fulfill his destiny as clown, Philo was required to experience the extremes of his life. For it is in the extremes that the clown learns about that secret place where hearts are touched and humanity healed, for only those who can make others laugh must first truly understand what it means to cry.

To touch a heart, to understand there is a heart, to care, that is what makes the clown so special. For the clown is and has always been the great healer...and so it is with Philo.

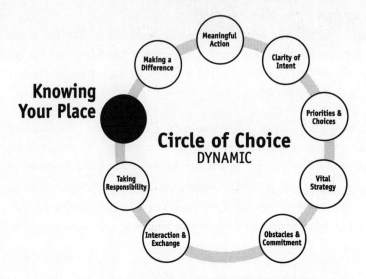

You can only make a difference
if you find your place

The **Entrepreneurial Traits** that need to be
developed and expanded here are:

_____

RESOURCEFULNESS
using your networks and your skills to communicate what you have to offer

_____

WILLINGNESS TO LEARN
to try new ways and to make mistakes

_____

COURAGE
to go to that place that is not comfortable and face the unknown on your own behalf

_____

KNOWING YOUR PLACE

Philosophy

You have come to an understanding about your skills, competencies and limitations as well as your definition of meaningful work for you. Having acquired this objective self-knowledge, you are now better prepared to know where you fit in.

This phase of the process is all about being the right person in the right place at the right time. It is about not having to pretend that you fit into a position. It is about not becoming distracted from what you consider important. It is about looking beyond...where can you, your talents and your interests best serve and best fit?

It is not simply about moving up, but rather where you best fit in. Here it is not about title or position as much as it is about the art of placement. Networking, understanding connections, timing and "know-how" are all key to this phase in your personal Career Management.

Links

⚹ Career management, whether done from within an organization or otherwise, requires fore-sightedness, tenacity, engine power, self-directedness, self-knowledge, work ethic, energy, purposefulness, vision, self-confidence and persistence and a sense of the proactive. These are many of the qualities that have to be nurtured and developed in a successful career management strategy.

⚹ In this phase it is now time to launch you and apply some of the entrepreneurial skills you have been developing and try them out on the world.

⚹ You need to remember that career management is for life and so, put in that framework, you will always be moving through the Circle of Choice Dynamic. There is never a time when you shouldn't be vigilant. If the job is looking rosy, then use the "up times" to make connections, network, work your contacts, find out what's going on in the industry, etc. When challenging times come your way, as they assuredly will, you will have a backlog of information and connections to tap into.

Ish, you know I've done a lot of work on career management issues - but this step is too much for me. You are asking me to do the thing I abhor above all else and that is to sell. I don't want to do it...it is too hard, I don't know how and I really find this whole approach pretty boring.

Well, I can hear how all of this is affecting you and I do understand your feelings about selling. Selling has become a bad word in today's world but communicating your value and your worth to others is quite different from selling. It is about getting you out in the world, connecting with the right people so you can discover where you best fit.

In practical terms, probably you've not done many cold calls or had much experience at working your network. What you now need is some guidance and encouragement to do just that. Practicing scripts and rehearsing what needs to be said is very important here. This is where your mentor could be invaluable as he or she quite probably has more experience executing this step than you. You will find their involvement invaluable.

 # Fables and Fairy Tales...
a story for every step of the way on The Circle of Choice Dynamic

The person for whom *Living Cat's Nine Lives* was written had this to say about their story. (When Dalcon was born, she was given the same name as her deceased brother.)

"Insights into who I am and what I am capable of."

> "Very touching. It's an intimate thing. It's nice to have someone care that much to want to do it."

> "Yes, it resonates. It changes every time it is read. Different feel. Seemed valid."

> "Going back in the past when it's written - it is more concrete in writing."

"Yes, it is more the way it is written - the attitude in the story. A different way of looking at my life."

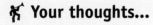 **Your thoughts...**

☗ *Living Cat's Nine Lives* ☗

She was sleek and silent and mostly serene. She moved through her world with ease, maneuvering strange lands, worlds that others were not even aware existed. And like her feline friends, this cat made sure she got what she needed, but learning this skill had taken a lifetime…one of many?

Her name was Dalcon…not who she was…not who she wasn't just in between not the heir but the replacement heiress who would always resist the legacy. How do you replace what can never be? You become other…there but never there. Already marked in stone as no more, yet very much of this world.

So where does one find oneself and how do they proceed? Dalcon knew from an early age that she was everything that was not wanted. There was no acceptance of who she was, so she disassociated…well wouldn't you? People trying to save your soul, a borrowed soul…your soul…it didn't seem to matter, just save it! And Dalcon said NO! "I will do it my way or it won't get done"…and it almost didn't.

No friends or one friend at a time of such a singular nature that they stood the test of time, for a time but not the test of time. How could they? She was always changing, growing, testing, tempting fate. "They will not hold me down…or back…or accountable for their beliefs. I will see how other people live…they think I'm an angel? Let them! I will experience life so I KNOW, not what 'they' say but my truth."

With grit and determination she crafted her way…she made plans, she laid a foundation. She was committed to finding her heart's desire…and she did. The creativity of art and thought, energy and healing were brilliantly integrated into her many lives. And what of the other whose name was Dalcon's? One wonders whether the other in fact supports her creative artistry, an artistry that manifests as she nurtures the lives of others. Diminutive as she might be, when required she has the power of…TEN? Perhaps that explains her capacity for love, for caring and for mysteries… always mysteries.

Dear one, nurtured by the gift of grace, our heroine Dalcon has been able to accept the reality of her unwanted presence in the past and changed her presence in the present, to a gift of great worth for the future. Life, reality and love have been nourished and kindled by Dalcon's hope…and remember always, hope is the promise of the future without expectation.

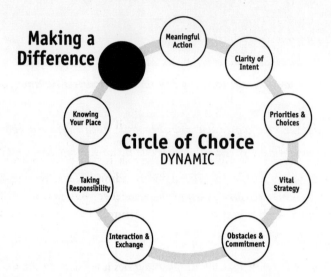

Making a Difference

Meaningful Action

Clarity of Intent

Priorities & Choices

Circle of Choice
DYNAMIC

Vital Strategy

Obstacles & Commitment

Interaction & Exchange

Taking Responsibility

Knowing Your Place

In this space you are making a signature statement
about who you are and what your work
means to you at the deepest level.

The **Entrepreneurial Traits** that need to be
developed and expanded here are:

_____

FEARLESSNESS AND PROACTIVENESS
making choices to make things happen

_____

RISK-TAKING
being willing to step up to the plate and give what you have to offer…regardless

_____

EMOTIONAL INTELLIGENCE
you can relate with others and see where you fit

_____

EFFORT
a willingness to do what is needed to be done

_____

MAKING A DIFFERENCE

Philosophy

Meaningful work is about feeding your spirit, your essence and if it is not feeding your spirit, then you would not class it as meaningful. This is a powerful place of doing. You have a sense that you are where you should be. You want to make a contribution and the risk is that your contribution will not be accepted. This space involves being accepted, received and/or admitted into the bigger picture. In the bigger picture, making a difference is a larger than life experience. Relationship with others is very important and everyone involved feels a part of the bigger picture. The experience is very attractive to everyone because individual egos have no place here.

This experience does not necessarily come automatically. Nor does it necessarily come without effort and risk. Here you are called to make proactive choices in order to make things happen. To do this you must be aware of what is happening, and be able to relate to others as a means of seeing where you fit in to the total picture.

To get what you really want requires that you be prepared to take a chance and do, so you can become who you are relative to the work that you wish to be doing.

Links

Whether you are attempting to find meaning in what you are already being paid to do, searching for work in your current organization or contemplating going to a new organization…you will want to choose how you wish to frame this new work experience and make the choices necessary to make that happen.

> 🏃 To help you focus on what would be meaningful, go to *Managing My Perspective* and review the Meaningful Work Indicators Assessment. This exercise will give you a good sense of what has and has not been meaningful for you in work.

> 🏃 Choose a growth and development task from your Personal Development Action Plan at the conclusion of *Managing My Development*. Decide how you are going to make this happen. Be specific.

You know, Ish, it sounds good to want to make a difference, but it is just not practical where I work. They say they want us to be empowered, but every step of the way is a major fight. The boss wants to be in control and that's it. It just doesn't seem possible that I can make a difference.

Your frustration is very clear. I would say that this is where being entrepreneurial would be helpful. You have to decide how you want to address the trust issue on the part of your employer and in the process you will want to determine what that lack of trust might be about and how it is affecting you.

Maybe you are not presenting the available options to your boss in the most effective way to instill the level of trust needed. Maybe no way will ever be good enough. Just assessing what is wrong is an important step. If it is something you are doing wrong or not approaching correctly, then figure out what you can do about it. If it is unsolvable, make a decision or two about what you will do about it.

Now might be the time to look for other positions in or out of your company or perhaps a course to make you more marketable. Either way you will feel better because you have made a decision to move. Whatever you do, I encourage you not to feel that it is hopeless. You will just become stuck in feeling sorry for yourself or possibly immobilized from anger or fear. Remember, this Circle of Choice Dynamic is about change, energy and movement... and it works.

Fables and Fairy Tales...

a story for every step of the way on The Circle of Choice Dynamic

The person for whom *Stardust Nymph* was written had this to say about their story.

"(It says) we all have a story...and goes against the worldview that only big people are important" (enough to have a story).

"It is important to live a life with a mythical quality. It should be that my life is a hologram of a myth and I am the center of the universe, if I live my life within that myth."

"It felt like being given a precious gift. It was inspiring...if someone saw that in me, it gives me hope. Helped me celebrate my life. Can I accept my special-ness? Do I try and pass for ordinary? Why can't I dance with what dances through me?"

⚐ Your thoughts...

✗ *Stardust Nymph* ✗

Before the dawn of time when Earth as we know it was yet a promise to be fulfilled, there flourished a magical world just past the planet Venus, cradled lovingly in a cushion of stars. Now in this world, which was called Tejg, there lived all manner of faeries and sprites. It had been foretold that a new planet was being formed and that when it was ready a select few would be allowed to go to this new place called Earth and live a life as if they were one of them.

Now among all those who waited was one named Crystal, a deliciously sensuous nymph who desired to live, truly live a life that would, like her name, have sharp edges, clarity and power. She wanted to be a protector of the downtrodden and a conduit to the Presence of that which she knew to be greater than her and all others.

Living among the stars was such a wonderful place to be, so one might wonder why Crystal had such a deep desire to go to Earth. It was the fascination of the beyond. Beyond held the mystery and the promise of what could not be realized where you are. Tejg was home, the known and all that warmed Crystal's heart. But the unknown…now that was where life was really lived.

And in its time Earth came into being and Crystal took her place with those who would go to Earth. Packing her kit with an abundance of stardust, she joyfully left her cushion of stars in search of the beyond. And the years went by. Her life on Earth was fruitful. She gave much of herself to others and undertook the arduous yet captivating journey of self-discovery with tenacity and purpose. And through it all she never forgot her desire for the beyond. For in striving to discover self through the beyond, she did that which we are all asked to do…remember who we are, why we are here and how we can be of service to our fellow travelers.

Daily Crystal glows and grows with a sense of hope, for always she believes that hope and the beyond make good companions on her journey…if you will, a star to set her course by.

Meaningful Action

Circle of Choice
DYNAMIC

- Making a Difference
- Clarity of Intent
- Priorities & Choices
- Vital Strategy
- Obstacles & Commitment
- Interaction & Exchange
- Taking Responsibility
- Knowing Your Place

Life is passing you by

The **Entrepreneurial Traits** that need to be *developed and expanded* here are:

FLEXIBILITY AND ADAPTABILITY
these qualities keep you unstuck

WILLINGNESS TO LEARN
finding other ways of moving into your future

SENSE OF URGENCY
understanding and not losing sight of the fact that a dynamic career plan will always be important

Welcome change into your heart and yield to its rhythms. Birth hope and an imaginative mobility that will open you to your own creative vitality. What follows is ease and flow and a fluid work identity.

CAROL ANN GOTCH

MEANINGFUL ACTION

Philosophy

There is a tremendous pull for all of us to settle for the way things are. We don't want to put in the effort. At one point, perhaps when you were without work or threatened by the loss of a job or a major change, you promised yourself that this would never happen again. You said you would make sure that you continually managed your career so you would be prepared should change occur.

But you forgot. Inertia set in and you fell asleep. The circumstances of your life kept unfolding all around you, but you chose to ignore the road signs presented to you along the way. The issue here is that you want to sustain the momentum you have created. You want to stay awake and step into the flow of life. Being awake and more aware of what's going on around you creates a sense of harmony. It allows you to become who you are, who you can be, who you choose to be.

Meaningful Action suggests that you stay open for new things to happen. We are all part of the evolution and unfolding of life, so you don't want to miss the opportunities that are there just for you. The message here is that you want to make sure that you're not asleep when life comes a-callin'.

Links

The Spiral of Continual Growth and Learning in *The Entrepreneurial Way* is a key element in understanding how this process of Meaningful Action works in our lives.

> 🏃 *Managing My Approach* helps to explain how you can develop a sense of momentum and what the factors might be in your life currently, that are holding you back from creating this sense of momentum.

> 🏃 Continual use and reuse of the workbook itself, for purposes of assessment and reassessment, establish this process as a lifelong tool that should always be back of mind, as you pursue that which is meaningful.

> 🏃 Choose a growth and development task from your Personal Development Action Plan at the conclusion of *Managing My Development*. Decide how you are going to make this happen. Be specific.

You know, I've just come through a lot in the last couple of years. Quite frankly, I don't have time and I am too busy to even consider doing career management. Right now I am comfortable, I am getting a reasonable salary, the benefits are good, I feel settled and that's the way it is going to stay. And besides, what difference is anything I do going to make?

Well, it seems to me like you are as comfortable and settled as you can get...much more so and they will be checking to see if you still have a pulse. Be careful...sometimes this state is called stagnation.

Conversely, this place on the Circle is about movement and meaningful action. If you do not make some career plans for yourself in these times, you will have no plan in place to assist you when life takes you on your next ride into change, chance and chaos. Also know that it is in these unsettled places of change, chance and chaos, where, if you are ready, you can meet opportunity, and create your own good fortune.

That is what the Spiral of Continual Growth and Learning is about. To truly live your life, you are invited to engage in your own process of living. Stagnation is an option but the Path of Growth is the way of wholeness and well being.

 # Fables and Fairy Tales...

a story for every step of the way on The Circle of Choice Dynamic

The person for whom *Be a Sun My Man* was written had this to say about their story.

"I realized that I may be one of the people putting me down."

"I was surprised by the characters (in the story). The story made things clearer for me."

"felt discouraged that no one takes an interest in who you are."

"I think about it (the story) in relation to what does it mean for my future? To accomplish something...to change?"

"To me the biggest part - 'Sunny Boy you were never alone".

"Take the risk. Confirm that I am as good as the story says. I'm not alone. There are positives. I can dwell on the positives as easily as the negatives."

⚉ *Be a Sun My Man* ⚉

Long ago and far away in the Kingdom of The Possible, there lived a magical wizard. His name was Taranga. The King, whose name was Phedron, valued the guidance of Taranga above all others.

One day Taranga came to King Phedron and told him of a very special child who would shortly be born into the kingdom. "This child has such a special gift. It is as if his person will be made of musical thoughts and chords. He will be one of your majesty's greatest treasures." King Phedron was a good king and he truly believed that treasures were to be treasured. Thus he said to Taranga ,"Go to the about-to-be-born child and cast a spell, so my child's musical treasure will flourish and grow through a lifetime. "Taranga did as he was bidden and the baby boy child understood why he was born into the world at this time.

And the child grew. He was a dear little chap, a little ray of sunshine. Wherever he went in the kingdom, his music brought warmth and light. The world knew he was special and because he was such a cause of joy, he became known as 'Sunny Boy'. Unbeknownst to the boy, Taranga watched over him from a distance. The magic of the wizard spilled over into the young boy's life…until his seventh year. And then everything changed. There were all manner of Nonsters in the kingdom, who did not revel in the young boy's music. They despised it. They were jealous of him. They set out to silence him…to convince him that what he said and sang was of little worth. They were successful.

As the young boy grew, he forgot why he was here…he forgot Taranga's blessing. He could not remember, no matter how hard he tried, that he was one of King Phedron's greatest treasures. Sunny Boy's sun slowly grew dim. He went within. He doubted his worth. He walked alone. But Taranga had not deserted him and he blessed Sunny Boy with a special gift. "I give you the gift of perseverance…do not let your music die…for one day when it is time you will bring your music to the world to offer hope and many hearts will be healed…including your own. Sunny Boy, your sun will shine once more."

Dear reader, as is often true with those with very special gifts, they must endure a time, often a very long time of trial, pain and learning. This is done to ensure that when the time is right, that the gift has been honed, life's lessons have been learned and the true beauty of the gift can shine…for the benefit of humankind.

Sunny Boy, you were never alone. Taranga was always there and King Phedron always knew the true worth of your treasure. Become comfortable with who you are. When you make friends with your King and your Magical Wizard…you will bloom in the rays of your Sun.

2

MANAGING MY FUTURE

> NOTE: The questions asked here and elsewhere in this book are in SMALL CAPS. These questions could require lengthy answers. You will find it helpful to have a notebook or binder for recording your answers and charting your Work-Life path and progress through the years.

The format of Managing My Future leans heavily on personal introspection. What has been, what is and of course what could be…those are the questions. It challenges the reader to be very entrepreneurial in making observations, connections and conclusions. Designed to empower, it creates a climate that will encourage personal awareness, vision and choice…about what you want in your future.

To effectively manage anything is to be attentive to those aspects of the project that require attention on an ongoing basis…and that goes for managing your future as well. In the business of managing your future, there are things that need to be monitored and kept top of mind, with the same degree of care as one applies to dress or diet. Some of those might be:

- Create a vision of your future…energize your dream for you - often
- Find a mentor…your dream needs support and guidance
- Read about trends and how they affect you…upgrade continually
- Know your place…where you fit in your field of endeavor
- Develop ease of movement with change and transition
- Work on being more flexible, adaptable and willing to learn
- Develop the skills of being the leader of you
- Consider how well your personal and your career dreams integrate
- Other?

~ If you don't have a sense of where you're going, then anywhere will do ~

My Future - can I spare the time?

This exercise will help you see how much of your time has been spent in the last five years on constructively thinking about your future. You may have been very proactive, i.e. really keeping your eyes open, or for whatever reason you may have been reactive, i.e. letting the system, your company or your boss do it for you. Just know that there is always room for consciously focusing a bit more of your time and attention on what you think you want in your future. Even a bit of time could make such a big difference…and of course it is your life and you are worth it.

Please indicate the amount of time you have devoted to thinking constructively and proactively about the aspects on the left (as described above).

	1 hour/**week**	1hour/**month**	1 hour/**year**	1 hour/**5 years**
My vision	☐	☐	☐	☐
My mentor	☐	☐	☐	☐
Trends/upgrading	☐	☐	☐	☐
Where I fit	☐	☐	☐	☐
Ease with change	☐	☐	☐	☐
Open to what's new	☐	☐	☐	☐
Being leader of you	☐	☐	☐	☐
Integrated career/personal	☐	☐	☐	☐
Other	☐	☐	☐	☐

WHAT DO THE RESULTS TELL YOU? THINK ABOUT IT.

For a balanced approach, while you are considering this question of time spent, you might want to ask yourself how much time you spend worrying about your job security, the number of hours you work, the degree to which you are engaged in your work, your relationships at work and how your work is affecting your life at home, etc.

When you look at the big picture, if you are spending a lot of time being anxious and worried, you might consider giving up some of this time investment to a more constructive investment of your time...devoted to your future. It could help you create the space you need to fashion some much-needed wins for yourself, your career and your family.

Taking Stock

Many of the questions in this section will require some thought, some self-remembering and some self-observing. If your answers don't come to you at one sitting, that's just fine. The richness of your answers is enhanced by as many details of your story as you can remember. The same will be true later on, as you flesh out the richness of your dream.

Your career

DO YOU FEEL YOUR CAREER IS ON TRACK?

WHAT SKILLS HAVE YOU ACQUIRED OVER THE SPAN OF YOUR CAREER?

ARE THERE CERTAIN TECHNICAL COURSES, SOFT SKILLS TRAINING, ETC. YOU'VE BEEN MEANING TO DO TO FURTHER YOUR CAREER? WHAT ARE THEY? AS YOU GO THROUGH THIS PROCESS, DO YOU STILL THINK THESE ARE RELEVANT, OR CAN YOU SET SOME OF THEM ASIDE?

WHAT HAVE YOU REALLY ENJOYED?

AS YOU THINK ABOUT IT, CAN YOU SEE ANY THREADS THAT RUN THROUGH YOUR CAREER EXPERIENCE?

DOES WHAT YOU DO NOW HAVE ANYTHING TO DO WITH WHAT YOU WANTED TO BE WHEN YOU WERE LITTLE? (REALLY THINK ABOUT THIS - YOU MIGHT BE SURPRISED.)

ANYTHING ELSE?

As you look over your musings, how does where you have been impact where you are going? This is worth some thought. Building on your past accomplishments, experience and yearnings is a very important part of managing your future.

 ~ This is what the Spiral of Continual Growth and Learning is about...it helps you see the big picture of you life and where and how things fit together ~

Integration of career and personal life

This exercise is about choices. Once again it is designed to make you think, to ask questions and to ponder. This is about taking stock as you decide how you are going to manage your future. As you work with these questions, try to imagine what the obvious conclusion will be if you stay on your current trajectory. For example: "Having looked at how I am doing my worklife today, I will be able to say that I am consciously choosing not to be engaged with my family in the growing years. In other words, in twenty years I can say because of career choices I made, I chose to miss seeing my children grow up.".

Is there balance in the way you are living and working?

	Career/Work	Personal Life
meaningful	YES · SO-SO · NO	YES · SO-SO · NO
personally empowered	YES · SO-SO · NO	YES · SO-SO · NO
in line with my values	YES · SO-SO · NO	YES · SO-SO · NO
reasonable workload	YES · SO-SO · NO	YES · SO-SO · NO
family needs met	YES · SO-SO · NO	YES · SO-SO · NO
time for self, friends	YES · SO-SO · NO	YES · SO-SO · NO
stress	YES · SO-SO · NO	YES · SO-SO · NO
uncertain future	YES · SO-SO · NO	YES · SO-SO · NO
sufficient money	YES · SO-SO · NO	YES · SO-SO · NO
good relationships	YES · SO-SO · NO	YES · SO-SO · NO
functional system	YES · SO-SO · NO	YES · SO-SO · NO

Pause and reflect upon what you have recorded. NOTE: Not all YES's will indicate a strength nor NO's a weakness.

IF THE WORST WERE TO HAPPEN AND YOU WERE TO PREDICT THE ACHILLES HEEL IN YOUR EXISTING WORK-LIFE SYSTEM - WHERE WOULD IT BE?

Make note of this observation because it requires attention as you move into your future.

Other important questions

 ~ To know what is missing gives clues to what's needed in the future ~

...about my life in general

WHAT DO I NEED IN MY DAY THAT ISN'T THERE NOW? TIME FOR MYSELF, EXERCISE, TIME FOR RELATIONSHIPS...TIME TO THINK?

AM I TRYING TO DEVELOP THE WHOLE ME - HEAD, HEART, BODY, SPIRIT - OR IS THERE A PART(S) I CONSISTENTLY IGNORE?

WHAT DO I THINK ABOUT THE UNSPOKEN DEMANDS SOCIETY PUTS ON ME RELATIVE TO SUCCESS, MATERIALISM, RELATIONSHIPS AND HAPPINESS?

DO I QUESTION THESE SOCIETAL EXPECTATIONS FOR ME AND MINE?

WHAT MAKES ME HAPPY? DO I HAVE ANY IDEA WHAT I DREAM FOR MYSELF?

DO I STILL DREAM FOR MYSELF?

WHERE IN MY LIFE DO I FEEL I AM FREE TO MAKE CHOICES? WHY?

WHERE IN MY LIFE DO I FEEL I AM NOT FREE TO MAKE CHOICES? WHY?

WHY AM I HERE? DO I FEEL THAT THERE IS PURPOSE TO MY EXISTENCE AND IF SO, WHAT WOULD THAT PURPOSE BE?

...about my work

AM I GOOD AT WHAT I DO, AND AM I FULLY ENGAGED WHEN I AM DOING IT...IN OTHER WORDS, IS MY WORK MEANINGFUL, DOES IT FEED THE ESSENCE OF WHO I AM?

DO I LIKE WHAT I DO? HOW LONG WILL I CONTINUE TO LIKE IT?

WHAT WOULD I LIKE TO DO NEXT? WHAT WOULD MAKE ME HAPPY?

IF I HAD A CHANCE TO CHANGE...WHAT WOULD I RATHER BE DOING THAN WHAT I'M DOING RIGHT NOW?

WHY DO I WORK? WHAT DOES WORK MEAN TO ME?

WHAT ARE SOCIETY'S EXPECTATIONS FOR ME RELATIVE TO WORK?

WHAT DO I THINK ABOUT THE CULTURE OF MY CURRENT WORKPLACE...ARE THE UNWRITTEN RULES CONSISTENT WITH MY VALUES AND BELIEF SYSTEM?

WHAT WOULD THE IDEAL WORKPLACE CULTURE LOOK LIKE?

DO I NEED AN ATTITUDE ADJUSTMENT REGARDING THE CONCEPT OF WORK AND MY CURRENT JOB IN PARTICULAR?

Who is steering your ship?

AM I LIVING IN THE LAND OF CHOICE, CHANCE AND OPPORTUNITY? WHEN I DECIDE IT IS TIME TO MAKE A MAJOR CAREER CHANGE OR ANY OTHER IMPORTANT DECISION ASSOCIATED WITH WORK…WHERE DO MY SIGNALS COME FROM? FROM INSIDE MYSELF, FROM OUTSIDE MYSELF, OR DO I TAKE THE PATH OF LEAST RESISTANCE AND LET IT GET MADE FOR ME?

DOES THE VOICE INSIDE ME CHOOSE WHAT

- ☐ I desire
- ☐ I know is ethically correct
- ☐ resonates with my principles
- ☐ works for me personally
- ☐ blends with my family values
- ☐ other?

DO THE VOICES OF OBLIGATION, EXPECTATION AND CONFORMITY TELL ME TO CHOOSE WHAT

- ☐ pays the most
- ☐ is what 'they say' is the best decision
- ☐ has the most power and prestige
- ☐ will compromise my principles
- ☐ suits my agenda but doesn't consider the family's needs
- ☐ other?

DO I BECOME FROZEN WITH FEAR, LULLED BY APATHY OR STUCK IN A PATTERN OF DECISION AVOIDANCE?

DO I JUST WAIT IT OUT, KNOWING THAT IF I REFUSE TO TAKE THE RESPONSIBILITY THAT IS RIGHTFULLY MINE, I CAN'T IN THE END BE HELD RESPONSIBLE IF THE DECISION TURNS SOUR?

DO I FIND THIS WORKS FOR ME BECAUSE I CAN ALWAYS BLAME THE WAY MY LIFE HAS UNFOLDED ON CIRCUMSTANCE, BAD LUCK OR POOR TIMING?

 ~ These questions probably need to be considered over time, and fleshed out as new insights and observations come to you. It should paint a very clear picture of how you are integrating your career and personal life management at the present time ~

There is more to *Managing My Future* than developing your Strategic Career Plan for the time you will spend in the workforce. What about when you retire? Many people do a good job of focusing on financial requirements. It is not often, however, that people focus on their own happiness. It seems they believe that by default, money will take care of that.

This section asks - what do you really want to do when you leave the workplace? Many people focus on activities, a 'to do' list if you will of everything from travel, to hiking, to caring for the grandkids.

You are invited to consider another way. To come home to yourself…your dreams, your passions, and your idea of what you choose your future to hold for you. It is a most empowering approach. It begins by offering an opportunity for you to look at how you have handled life-changing decisions in your past.

I remember when...

This exercise is designed to help you remember some of the more significant major changes that have been related to your work and personal life in your past.

In high school
How did you choose the courses you took, the ones that defined what possible paths your career could take?

(Record if the research and decision-making process was done by you or by others. If others, who were they and what was their relationship to you? Were you engaged in the process or were you willing to do what you were told? Or perhaps you don't remember. Have any idea why you don't remember?)

Post-high school
How did you decide on the work you would do or which course of study you would follow?

In your personal life
When it came time to marry, how did you make that decision?

(Did you seek professional guidance, did events and expectations of others influence you or did it just happen?)

In the workplace
How have you managed your own career up until now?

(Consider how your career has progressed through the years you have been working. Have you paid attention to how you felt about your work or has it just been about being employed?)

What observations would you make about how you handled moments of change? Is there a pattern?

When you look back from your current vantage point, do you feel that your method of decision-making served you well?

If in retrospect you are not altogether pleased, what different actions could you have taken that would have served you better?

Retirement...transferring what has been learned

In our society, there has been a major rewrite of the life and living script over the last fifty years. Generally, we are living longer and retiring earlier. Conceivably we now have another twenty-five years...a span of time, almost another lifetime in our ancestors' terms, and that span of time will be ours to live. What a gift!

But so far it is a gift that has come almost entirely without instructions...like becoming a parent. Who told us that there might be a few things it would be helpful to know to go along with the little bundle? Do we know how to make this gift of life work for us? What the gift signifies is that each of us has a completely new opportunity, a 'one more chance' opportunity in this lifetime...to decide how we want to live out our days in a way that is meaningful to us.

The exercise you just completed about how you have made major life decisions in the past has been a wonderful opportunity for you to remember how you did it. You can now decide in the light of your past experience whether you want to do it differently this time round.

This 'looking at your retirement years' part of your entrepreneurial quest can be done on an ongoing basis in partnership with the other initiatives that you follow in this book. Depending on your age, the topic of retiring will naturally be more top of mind. Whatever your age there is nothing wrong with dreaming about what would be meaningful to you. Research possibilities and then try some of your ideas on for size. Knowing that you are investing in your dream is not only a good strategic approach but you will find it very energizing.

Begin to see your life as a continuum...the Spiral of Continual Growth and Learning. If you are able to do this, you will begin to see the interconnectedness of all parts of your life and how the longings of youth still wait to be heard but bringing those longings alive would benefit greatly from your experiences learned in the middle years.

Following is the story of *The Forgotten Seed*. This story captures the concept of the ***continuum of a life***. Your forgotten seed...your heart's desire has never left you, but it can get buried very deeply...almost to the point of being lost forever. But retirement is a time when you can express that long forgotten desire, maybe not as you would have in your teens and twenties, but in a richer way, a way that uses the nourishment of a lifetime of experience to bring forth the flowering of your youthful desires...in a whole new way that is uniquely yours.

❈ *The Forgotten Seed* ❈

There was a young child who, at a very early age, was happily playing in his backyard one day, when he discovered an object lying on the ground. It was a strange object, way too big for a little tyke like him to even hold in his wee small hands. Undaunted, he kept walking around and around this awesome 'what's it'. He didn't know what 'what's it' was and he didn't want to break the spell by calling Mom.

He leaned over. There were these strange ropes, very, very thin ropes and they looked a bit like the stuff his dad used on his fishing rod. He touched one rope. It made a sound. His heart raced. He touched another. It made a sound but it was a different sound. He could not believe his ears. He ran his whole little hand across all the thin ropes and he heard a wonderful sound - a chord of music. He was enchanted, inspired and alive. He was so excited. It was so special. It was as if a seed was sown in his garden that day. For as little as he was, he knew from that moment on, he would devote his life to music, sing songs and be famous. He knew in his heart, he would always want to feed his soul…as it had been fed in that moment.

And the days went by. He would wake each morning and race outside. He would sing and play his day away in a musical world of his own creation. For now these creations were in his heart and his imagination…the real music would come later. And so he grew, never losing his love of music…a natural, really, who had instantly recognized his giftedness, one day long ago, in his little garden.

And the years went by and soon it was time to work. And he said, "I want to play…my music, that will be my work"… and they said, because they were afraid and did not understand his gift - "get a real job' - and he did because it seemed to make sense and Father knows best, doesn't he? He went to work in a bank.

And the years went by. He certainly remembered his music. How could he forget? But something strange had begun to happen. He and his music were no longer one…for they had split. He no longer believed in himself and in bringing his music to the world. Instead he went to work where the world came to him…for money. And his music? Well, it was done on weekends and it did not flow as it once had. It was becoming harder and harder to bring forth those golden notes, for he had been silenced…by life and work. With no hope and a forgotten seed, he was a very unhappy man indeed.

And the years went by. He hopes no more. He exists in a world that is a far cry from the dream world of the little lad who planted his musical seed so long ago. But there is good news, for you see dear ones, he is not done. It is only the world that has told him so, just like his father told him to "get a real job" when he was a very young man. It is just that the myth that has taken root this time is that it is over…that he has missed his chance.

But what if it isn't over? What if it is just beginning? What if all these years he has been getting ready, building his experience, honing his skills and making the connections he will now need?

And where is the meaning in this story? Why, our hero has a choice. He can live out his last years of work in joyless unhappiness…or as he works each day, he can plan a future that is rooted in what he loves. He can look after the dream of the most important person in his world…himself. He can finally, after all these years, take heart and find the courage to nurture and grow his forgotten seed.

Other thoughts...

3

MANAGING MY APPROACH

All manner of wisdom

This section is filled with all manner of wisdom that is available to you on an "as needed" basis. There are many ways of looking at what it takes to find the energy to move and why finding that energy to move is so important. Somewhere on these pages of *Managing My Approach* you will find that one phrase, that one word, that one idea that will give you hope and spur you on to that which is meaningful for you.

 ~ It is comforting, it is real and it is the truth ~

The Energy of Attraction

Have you ever put off doing something...you don't know why, you just do? You put it off and put it off and one day you wake up and...it is time. You can't do it fast enough. Where once there was no energy to move, all of a sudden nothing can hold you back. Like, for instance, choosing to find out what you really want from life.

Choosing to find out what you want from life may seem daunting. But if you are attracted to the idea of doing and being what is meaningful to you, just stay with that feeling of attraction. Attraction creates its own energy. Over time, you are likely to move in the direction of that attraction.

What you think, what you want, what you believe and what is meaningful to you are important. If it becomes important enough, you will begin to move in the direction of that which is attractive to you. Little by little, your interest will begin to grow. Be gentle with yourself...remember, all good things take time...and what could be better than taking time for you?

Life Through A Wide-Angle Lens

When we can only see our own story up close, we lack perspective. We can't see where we have come from or where we might be going. Observing the lives of others is very enlightening for it gives us a chance to view a lifetime through a wide-angle lens. And what we see is that what seemed like a gifted life with many bright spots and high points, is realistically a life framed by all the challenges that the life fully lived can bring. One sees through the lives of others that in the lows we are groomed for the thrill of the highs and having been thus enticed, are seductively lured to take the ride back down, a ride that can often take our breath away. Everything and everybody experiences the ride. It is our railing against the flow of the ride that makes the flow not flow, creates fear and slows down what could be a very exciting and rewarding experience. In truth, hitting bottom is the good news, for bottom gives us something to push up from, energy if you will, to come back. The folks who are in real trouble are the ones who never hit bottom. No acceptance of what's happened, no energy to move forward, just a belief that once again they have been tricked by destiny. The lives of the great ones would tell us that this frame of mind above all else is illusion.

~ Paying attention to the stories of others is hugely important. It helps us see that we all are as one in the human journey ~

YOU and Wakening the Work-Life Warrior Within

Why is it that people who have major setbacks will tell you later in their lives that it was the best thing that ever happened to them? It is as if over time they came to view the unexpected change as an invitation and an opportunity rather than an intrusion. They were pushed by life and so they had to make a choice whether or not they would land on their feet. I think it can be harder when we are not given a push because it means that we have to give ourselves a push and that's a very hard exercise in awareness, vision and choice. Over time it is easy to get used to a negative situation…it can creep up on us. It is very difficult to say - enough is enough. A big thing constitutes a push. We can just adjust and adapt to little things. Often Career Management is dictated by the job you have, the promotions you get or the pink slips you receive. Not many people proactively pursue what they truly want to do or be. Rarely do people have a dream or a vision, although in truth not having a dream makes it difficult. It makes you feel more of a victim to where you are than a traveler on your own journey. It is so freeing to have an idea of what you want to be…what would be meaningful work for you. Maybe it will take some years to get there, but you can conduct your work-life with purpose. You can take courses and all manner of experiences will be there to enrich your dream rather than just being part of the work-life drudgery.

Dreams Take Time, Patience and Tenacity

Do we unconsciously short-circuit our dreams? You know, the ones that we dream for ourselves? Let's call them life-dreams. By their nature they are so much more than can be imagined in the moment and the power of these dreams is enormous…and when nurtured, they will unfold with time. Allowing for that time takes patience and tenacity and when you push it, the chances are pretty good that you will meet resistance. It is as if a force is saying, not that…just wait. It is not time.

As your dream unfolds, you will find there are setbacks. But you will also find over time that the setbacks on your dream journey are instructive. They teach you about you. And what you learn is often what you will need to know to take next steps or move forward sometime in the future. And there will be pitfalls…for promises of money, power and security are alluring and fear of failure can be overwhelming. But know that if you settle, your wonderful dream will be frozen in time and its full potential will never be realized.

So if you have such a life-dream, and hopefully you do, hold it to your heart. Share it with those you love and trust. Pursue it, but do not become too riveted on outcome…for that would be like writing the ending without allowing the story to unfold.

Work-Life Balance

The Emperor's New Clothes is a tale for our times. The young child challenged the prevailing world-view...a view based on an agreed-upon illusion that the Emperor was dressed in his finery whereas in truth he was naked.

What if there was such a young child looking at work-life balance in today's society...the way we work, the way we spend, the way we do family, the way we do time, the way we do ourselves? Perhaps the wise young child would tell us we are very exposed. Should we consider finding another way?

But you can't create a new way if you keep doing things in the old way. If you insist on the old way, you limit the possibilities that the future holds for you. Know that it is important to validate the old ways, but understand that to move forward, it is necessary to create something new.

 ~ It is time to act like the child. Be the Conscious Leader of You...wake up and don't settle ~

Conscious Leadership

The Conscious Leader knows that if you continually look for problems, problems are what you will find. If you can take an appreciative look at your Work-Life situation, the possibilities are more likely to become apparent. This process takes a conscious effort on your part but is well worth the effort.

Awareness is vital to becoming the leader of you. To do this requires that you first "see", then create a vision of how your Work-Life could look if changes were made, then decide how you will make these changes.

Step 1: Take time to think about you and your Work-Life.
Examining and reflecting are first steps to creating AWARENESS. The only way you will truly understand the present is to take time, time to observe what happened in the past from your current vantage point - the present. If you currently experience stress, anxiety and a sense of life being less than meaningful, there is no reason to believe this situation will improve...unless you are prepared to examine the patterns and influences that brought you to where you are today.

Step 2: Appreciating that things can be different for you.
Create a VISION of what could be. It is true that your Work-Life is often complicated and difficult. It is also true that because of attitude and approach, life is often more difficult and complicated than it needs to be. We can get ourselves into a way of living or a pattern of behavior that is not conducive to a Work-Life that contributes to our well-being and wholeness.

Step 3: **Take steps to make your Work-Life more nurturing to you.**

It is important and life-giving to feel valued and respected, to do work that is meaningful and to live a Work-Life that is rich and nurturing. As a Conscious Leader you could begin by considering an appreciative approach to your life...seeing possibilities where you now see problems and abundance where once you saw scarcity. You will be amazed what just thinking appreciatively can do. Try it...you won't be disappointed.

A conscious choice for hope

Reach within yourself and find that place where your fears and hope meet and make a conscious choice for hope!

Energy
Movement

HOPE

Responsibility   **Creative Visioning**
Awareness   Visualize options

This triangle identifies the aspects in our work lives that represent hope. It no doubt applies to your personal life...think about it. The issues here are:

Responsibility...involves awareness, seeing what is actually happening. You might be saying "I hate this job", but you would also be saying "What am I going to do about it?" ..."I'll take action", "I'll upgrade my skills and expand my network, I'll decide if I need to adjust my attitude."

Energy...involves movement, what I am doing. It will be reflected in comments such as "I don't have a job but I'm conducting a good job search," "I could lose my job so I'm upgrading my skills just in case," "I am being taken advantage of...I will be firm about my personal boundaries."

Creative Visioning ...you are able to visualize options that will allow you to be what you can be. "I know the world is changing and I am ever vigilant to opportunities," "I don't have a job but I look at possibilities" and "I stop focusing on what I cannot change and start to change the things I can."

Each spot on the triangle indicates a willingness to do, to be or to see. Ultimately hope defines our willingness to change and deal with the unknown.

~ We greatly restrict our personal capacity for hope if we are unable or unwilling to change ~

Applying aspects of the hope model can significantly help to dispel your fear and allow you to create an opening for future possibilities.

Three other factors that help your process:

Urgency
Change through choice

MOMENTUM

Risk
Decision-making & responsibility

Motivation & Commitment
Self-confidence & Know-how

The issues are:

🚶 **Risk**...is seeing your role in taking personal responsibility for the decisions that you choose to make.

🚶 **Urgency**...is making a choice to make a change by putting one foot in front of the other and doing what needs to be done.

🚶 **Motivation and Commitment**...is exhibiting the self-confidence and know-how to be the best that you can be!

Working this triangle gives you plenty of room for maneuvering...to see, to be and to do. A good way of building momentum.

~ Don't spin your wheels. Maintain a balance between risk, urgency and motivation and commitment. This will help you overcome feelings of inadequacy, lack of focus, and the tendency to want to give up...all natural reactions when these three are not working in balance ~

Risk

Risk is coming face to face with the unknown. The unknown is also what we fear for if we knew everything about it...it wouldn't be a risk.

Risk could be viewed as fear's twin and when they walk hand in hand they supply energy to each other for good or ill. In certain situations, fear and risk can inspire us and spur us on to greater heights and in other situations the fear/risk combination can immobilize us.

Three types of risk:

RECKLESS ABANDON: This is when you just jump in, you don't consider the consequences, and you just do it. This type of risk is fraught with danger because you haven't taken the time to examine your options, i.e. quitting a job when you're mad and don't have another one to go to.

CALCULATED: This is where you think out your options, examine the upside and downside of the situation and then make your move.

FROZEN: This is when you worry the risk to death and never make a move one way or another.

 ~ Risk is necessary if we are going to move because when we move we don't know what place we are going to...and that is just a part of life ~

Risk Tolerance Assessment

To assess your risk tolerance, review the following attributes. These attributes help you to measure how badly you want something and what you are prepared to do to make what you want happen.

First, read the following definitions. Get a good sense of what these definitions really mean to you and how these attributes manifest in your life relative to career management, job search or other work-related transition issues.

ENERGY: the very essence of what you present to the world. Your life force, your vitality, your engine quality

SELF-DIRECTION: the level of personal commitment you have to making the things happen that you believe will guide you into your future in a positive manner

FOCUS: the ability to pinpoint your direction and adapt along the way as events and circumstances unfold

SELF-EVALUATION: the mindset and the skill to continually observe your own performance without the process becoming self-critical

SELF-CONFIDENCE: the sense of self-worth and self-esteem you require to present yourself and your ideas with confidence and your willingness to do what is necessary to create that level of confidence

WORK ETHIC: the capability to do what has to be done and the willingness to do it

TIME MANAGEMENT: the desire and the ability to devise appropriate methods of using your time that will allow you to complete your personal goals

TENACITY: the ability to not necessarily take no for an answer. To hold to your truth and to what is important to you

PERSEVERANCE: the ability to stick at it long after everyone else has gone home and understanding that no's are just stepping stones and not brick walls

DISCERNMENT: the wisdom to know when your qualities of tenaciousness and perseverance need to be redirected.

 ~ Boy, these are important ~

Completing the exercise

When completing the exercise you will be offered two options. "*On the back burner*" suggests that you might very well have good potential in each area but you have not turned your potential into reality.

"*Highly utilized*" suggests that this is an attribute for which you have flair: you use it well and it is an integral part of your life.

In this exercise you will examine the ten factors that a) influence to what degree you are able to assume risk and b) to understand how long you can sustain risk taking.

Risk Tolerance Assessment

	ON THE BACK BURNER	HIGHLY UTILIZED
Energy	1 · 2 · 3 · 4 · 5 · 6 · 7 · 8 · 9 · 10	1 · 2 · 3 · 4 · 5 · 6 · 7 · 8 · 9 · 10
Self-direction	1 · 2 · 3 · 4 · 5 · 6 · 7 · 8 · 9 · 10	1 · 2 · 3 · 4 · 5 · 6 · 7 · 8 · 9 · 10
Focus	1 · 2 · 3 · 4 · 5 · 6 · 7 · 8 · 9 · 10	1 · 2 · 3 · 4 · 5 · 6 · 7 · 8 · 9 · 10
Self-evaluation	1 · 2 · 3 · 4 · 5 · 6 · 7 · 8 · 9 · 10	1 · 2 · 3 · 4 · 5 · 6 · 7 · 8 · 9 · 10
Self-confidence	1 · 2 · 3 · 4 · 5 · 6 · 7 · 8 · 9 · 10	1 · 2 · 3 · 4 · 5 · 6 · 7 · 8 · 9 · 10
Work ethic	1 · 2 · 3 · 4 · 5 · 6 · 7 · 8 · 9 · 10	1 · 2 · 3 · 4 · 5 · 6 · 7 · 8 · 9 · 10
Time management	1 · 2 · 3 · 4 · 5 · 6 · 7 · 8 · 9 · 10	1 · 2 · 3 · 4 · 5 · 6 · 7 · 8 · 9 · 10
Tenacity	1 · 2 · 3 · 4 · 5 · 6 · 7 · 8 · 9 · 10	1 · 2 · 3 · 4 · 5 · 6 · 7 · 8 · 9 · 10
Perseverance	1 · 2 · 3 · 4 · 5 · 6 · 7 · 8 · 9 · 10	1 · 2 · 3 · 4 · 5 · 6 · 7 · 8 · 9 · 10
Discernment	1 · 2 · 3 · 4 · 5 · 6 · 7 · 8 · 9 · 10	1 · 2 · 3 · 4 · 5 · 6 · 7 · 8 · 9 · 10

MY TOTAL (out of 100) = _____

Scoring

1-25	You need to take a close look at what is happening for you. Have you thrown up your hands in frustration or are you not even present?
26-50	You have some stronger aspects of risk-taking that will be a resource. Take special note of which aspects are your strengths and build on them.
51-75	You have a high level of risk-taking in your life. You have a good sense of yourself and what you have to offer.
76-100	You know what you are about. You are very clear on who you are and where you are going. However, be aware that your determination and drive might overpower others.

This will help put into context each component of risk-taking and you can evaluate where you stand today. Are there aspects of risk-taking that are "highly utilized" in your daily life? Are there areas that might be on the "back burner" and may hold you back from moving effectively? And how does this impact your personal life? An important question!

Each of these attributes is a very important aspect of what is needed to follow the Entrepreneurial Way. Check the entrepreneurial traits that are needed at each spot on the Circle of Choice Dynamic. This will help put what is required at each step of the process into context.

Urgency

Urgency and risk go hand in hand. Our fear of taking risks can be offset by our sense of urgency. You know you wouldn't attempt lifting a 1,500-pound piece of concrete. The risk to your back would be monumental. But there are stories about people who have lifted such a weight when it was pinning down a child. For them, when the urgency increased, the risks relative to back injury were no longer a factor.

We always have "good intentions" when it comes to thinking about making changes, taking new directions or making choices. It is the taking action to make it happen that is difficult. Urgency is plain and simply about doing it. If you were saving the child, you are not going to stop in midair and wonder whether you should be holding the concrete. You just do it.

What often influences us is a sense of urgency or whatever is "pushing" us into taking the action. The Entrepreneurial Way is about creating your own sense of urgency. It is important in career management to muster up a sense of urgency on your own behalf…even without a crisis. Urgency will help you execute your plan and move your process forward.

Motivation and Commitment

Motivation and commitment are the drivers that spur us on. We can easily spot the person who is motivated and committed to their task as well as the one who is not. It is hard to put your finger on these qualities, yet they are so visible, and so obvious…particularly when they are not present.

Some of us are more naturally motivated and committed; yet even the best of us have our moments when we really have to hunker down or we can easily lose our resolve. Motivation and commitment require our attention at all times so we don't become complacent.

These questions invite you think about times you were motivated and committed and times you were not. The important thing here is to tap into how each of these experiences felt for you. As you move forward in your career management process, you will want to remember good experiences that made you feel responsible and alive. It makes it easier if you can connect with and replicate the feelings associated with a positive experience.

Record any remembered experiences around these questions and focus on how you felt. If some don't fit, add your own.

WHEN HAVE YOU FELT TRULY MOTIVATED TO FURTHER A TASK BEYOND WHERE YOU ORIGINALLY PLANNED TO TAKE IT?

DO YOU REMEMBER A TIME WHEN YOU FELT YOU HAD STAYING POWER?

HAVE YOU EVER BEEN COMMITTED TO SOMETHING FOR ANOTHER PERSON? WHAT DID BEING COMMITTED FEEL LIKE IN THIS INSTANCE?

HAVE YOU EVER BEEN COMMITTED TO SOMETHING THAT WAS JUST ABOUT YOU? WHAT MADE THAT FEELING DIFFERENT?

OTHER?

Momentum

What you want to strive for is the blending and balancing of risk, urgency and motivation and commitment for the purpose of building and maintaining momentum. Whether real, or contrived by you to keep you moving, momentum propels you forward. That is a very important aspect of career management. Staying in the flow and not losing momentum is most important to your process.

When we are immobilized...it looks like this

I've got to be a success

easier to give up   what's the use   afraid to take a risk

I blame others I just don't care   Avoidance (TV!)   **FEAR**

Imbalance can create chaos   Eating habits change   Confidence down

STRESS Loss of purpose   **MENTAL SHUTDOWN**   I blame others

can't deal with the unknowns   Physical malaise

ANXIETY   afraid to take a risk   **FEAR**

Insomnia

Ineffective verbal presentation   hate my job and it is not fair

ANGER   driven by fear and despair

Forget appointments

I feel lost   **STRESS**

Wanting to be in control   **ANXIETY**   Sleeping in

MENTAL SHUTDOWN   Loss of focus

Stop sending resumes

Mental shutdown, I blame others,

afraid to take a risk   **ANGER**   Lower expectations

Greatly increase our capacity to be driven by fear and despair

MENTAL SHUTDOWN

I go limp, sense of immobilization,   Personal appearance goes

STRESS can't deal with the unknowns

Focus on entertainment   Loss of energy and enthusiasm

An unwillingness to do, to be or to see

Stress builds up for no reason

bogged down in not knowing who I am   Substance abuse Easily overwhelmed

Chores neglected

Guilt   Procrastination

Stay in house

Walking becomes wandering

Withdrawn   Defensive and irritable

I blame others

~ Even when you feel immobilized...some parts are still working. Use those parts now ~

As you work through this recognize that:

🏃 you are on a roller coaster ride and most of it feels downhill [don't form judgments about the ride... it is not good and it is not bad it is just an experience]

🏃 you do have choices

🏃 you need to connect with a person(s) with whom you can share your experience

~ One of the big temptations at this stage is to keep secret how you are feeling. Those who care about you probably are very aware of your pain, so hiding it is using up energy and is somewhat a dead end exercise. Expressing your feelings can help you to sort things through. In the pain, there might be something very important for you to learn. If you are open to this discovery, your experience could become a "jewel of a great price" ~

~ Give yourself a positive charge - whatever it takes to make you feel good about yourself. Change your pace by getting physically active - go for a walk, work out at the gym, etc. Make that list of positive traits and accomplishments when you're feeling good - look at it often. Spend time with someone who makes you feel good ~

~ Take a step back and reassess the big picture. Look at your life to see if you have balance - do you need to make more time for your family, friends, physical activity, mental or spiritual needs? Finding balance among the things that are important to you will give you more energy and resilience in the long run ~

~ Set a task for youself that is not too difficult, has a very defined time line and a very specific outcome. What you need now is a win...no matter how small ~

The Entrepreneurial Way...the hopeful way!

There will be times as you go through your lifelong career management process when discouragement will become your reality. Make no mistake, this is a common experience, but the skill you will need to learn is the ability to take a step back and recognize what's happening to you. You will want to learn what you need to help you address this challenge and change the situation. If you can't find the energy to do that, search out what's causing your energy to drain away from you. A good place to start is to revisit your dream, perhaps express it as a creative activity, to make it more real and less cerebral. This would also be a good time to re-clarify your intent.

Language is important

What we say to ourselves in our mind or to others out loud has a major influence on how we present ourselves or how others perceive and respond to us. Before you speak, be aware of how you are framing your thoughts because it's not only what you think, it is the way you express it that influences how others interpret your communication. Thus the tone and inflections in your voice become very significant.

Choose language to 'empower' your position

- Focus on I AM RESPONSIBLE and ACCOUNTABLE...
  Don't find fault and blame
- Focus on positive...I WILL WORK WITH
  Don't dwell on the down side...I can't change things
- Focus on constructive...I WILL TRY IT...
  Don't focus on conflict...it won't work
- Focus on consensus...I UNDERSTAND
  Don't focus on objection...I disagree
- Focus on decisive with...I KNOW
  Don't be passive with...I think
- Focus on...I WOULD BE GLAD TO
  Don't say...I have to
- Focus on reinforcing...I'M TRYING AND LEARNING
  Don't undermine with....I'm no good at
- Focus on....I TRIED AND LEARNED
  Don't dwell on...I failed
- Focus on...FROM NOW ON, I WILL
  Don't think about...If only I

Remember

How you deal with other people sets the tone for how they will deal with you!

 ~ Always know that life is a journey and you will travel easier if you just hop on board. A good attitude can make the ride a lot smoother ~

MANAGING MYSELF

Managing Myself helps you find the energy to search for meaningful work as well as learn how to facilitate your own growth process. You will learn how to release energy from your past and how to find energy in your dream for the future...wonderful tools to help you in your Career Management process.

 ~ Work-Life wellness means having your systems at an optimum state of wholeness and well-being, so you can handle what life sends you. Those systems would include but not be limited to your physical health, your emotional needs (having them resolved and/or understood), your training needs, your networks and your personal supports ~

Managing myself means knowing:

🏃 who I am, what makes me tick, what would meaningful work look like to me

🏃 how I am going to take all this information and make something happen

🏃 that I am important and that I must take the time to manage my life and my career the way I want it managed...if I want to reach the outcomes I desire

🏃 that I cannot leave it to someone else to make my decisions for me or to chart my life course and my career path

In the Chapter entitled *The Entrepreneurial Way* the Spiral of Continual Growth and Learning was presented as one of the basic precepts of this book. Simply put growth is a fact of life and if we can grasp what the patterns to growth are, we will be able to facilitate our own growing process.

If we can acknowledge and accept our history, we can avoid repeating patterns that got us into trouble in our past. We also can become aware that we can move out of or beyond our history by keenly observing the present and applying the appropriate skills to mold the future.

And further if we take the time to sort through the conditioning that we have received from parents, teachers, environment, friends, etc.we will be able to operate more clearly...knowing what our values are and what is truly important to us. Taking the time to do this and to create a vision, leads us to what is important for us in living out our life and our careers.

 ~ Remembering your history, the rich story that is your life, allows for visionary moments, moments when you can view the past, not as all bad or all good, but just as it is. For whatever your story, it got you where you are today. Telling your story allows you to observe those patterns and that process ~

WE HAVE TWO CHOICES... TO STAGNATE OR TO GROW

Path of stagnation

This is a review of what stagnation looks like:

- Letting my actions and movement be dictated by external circumstances
- Blaming others, the company for my personal fate…as if I have no personal responsibility in my own life
- Saying I have no choices
- Denying that the inevitable is going to happen
- Saying it won't happen to me

WHERE IN MY LIFE AM I FOLLOWING A PATH THAT STAGNATES MY GROWTH?

WHAT AM I WILLING TO DO ABOUT THAT?

Path of growth

Here is an expanded view of the Path of Growth sequence.

Comfort zones:

Life seems to be moving well - we're comfortable with career, relationships, etc. This is a good time to get comfortable and set in our ways!

Following the Entrepreneurial Way, you want to use this time of comfort to plan, to train and to network and whatever else you need to give you a sense that you are ready. It is a little like gathering your stores in late summer so that when winter comes, you have something to see you through.

Momentous events:

A crisis occurs. Either through choice or imposition, everything starts to change. This event can happen as a result of sickness, death, divorce, job loss, retirement, birthdays, moving out of the house, graduation, etc.

Think back in your own life when a crisis occurred. It is that moment when from that time on, nothing is the same. We don't always realize it at the time, but when we look back, we know it to be true.

Oblivion:

In this stage we protect or insulate ourselves from pain. This stage is characterized by emotional withdrawal, numbness, confusion and/or immobilization. We don't know where to turn. We know that we have to let go of the past - it is over, but on another level, clinging to some kind of security we hang on.

Transition occurs when you decide to let go and to mobilize yourself to move into the future. The past is part of your life - but you walk out of it - into the challenges of tomorrow. It's not easy - but it is the path of transition - it is the path of growth that works.

Exploring new horizons:

The next stage allows us to explore new solutions in our lives. This can take many forms: reading a book, discussions with friends or counselors, entering a program, etc. Make no mistake - it's not clear sailing - we are up and down in this stage. One moment things seem clear and another moment we are back to confusion and perhaps oblivion.

This is where the plans you have in place can kick in to help you through this difficult time. It will give you comfort, knowing you have some things in place to support your efforts.

Seizing the moment:

In this stage you may feel drained - but you begin to say: "I've got to decide." There may be many questions, for example "Is this right for me?" "Should I take the risk?" You take the risk and make the choices!

This is one of the places where chance and preparedness can come together…many people like to call it luck. In truth it is being ready when opportunity knocks.

 ~ We can often understand and see this path more clearly in other people's lives than our own. You will find that self-remembering how the Path of Growth has worked in your life in the past and self-observing what is happening right now in your life in the present could be most helpful ~

Releasing energy from the past

Just as a tree needs energy to grow and a car needs energy to run, we as human beings need energy to get us where we want to go now, today. This energy is not just about food, drink and sleep…it is about the will to want to.

If you are supporting feelings of anger, fear, resentment, shame, blame about how you have been treated in this job or by some boss or by life - in your recent past or long ago - you are using your precious energy to support those past feelings and events. Energy is a limited resource. If you use enormous energy to fund past hurts, you deplete your supply of energy to get you through today.

In your lifetime you have moved through the five "path of growth" stages many times as part of your human experience. But like all of us you hold on to past hurts and disappointments, and releasing them is very healthy.

Scripted fairy tale exercise

The following exercise is designed to help you release energy from the past. If you find it helpful, it is an exercise that you can do again and again. It entails writing a little fairy tale from a script that will be given to you. It will empower you to give healthy advice to "the you" in the past...and inspire "the you" of the present to a hope-filled future.

    🯅 Write your tale in the third person, as that is often easier and much more impersonal than in the first person. The fairy tale format will allow you to "write around" your energy-held memory and this should eliminate the necessity of cataloguing dates and times and who was right and who was wrong.

    🯅 Put the incident into the context of a lifetime...your lifetime. Putting it into perspective will help to lift the energy around it.

    🯅 Give those in your memory story only the amount of power they wielded then as opposed to the amount of power you are often willing to give them as you look back. You also have the capability of viewing the incident from the future.

    🯅 Offer sage advice to your character in the past and offer yourself the gift of hope for how this story can be resolved and put to rest in the future.

Here is your script. Follow the instructions/guidelines but take creative license to make your fairy tale your own.

To begin...choose a Where and When:

Long ago and far away...

Many years ago in the land of...

At the turn of the century in small town...

In the salt mines of Sanso in the middle years...

When luck chose wisely and...

On a dark and stormy night...

In an old Church lane by the sea...

In the darkness of the cave, Ibor rose...

Just east of Torbu in the reign of...

Such sadness came when...

On a lonely highway near...

Pain met joy on the road one day and...

Once upon a time...

When men were truly men and...

The times were ripe and never before...

Next...set the scene. Who are the characters - don't have too many or it will get too complicated.

a lonely child
a rich merchant
an angry gorilla
a silly spinster
a tattered old soul
a dangerous dragon
a magnificent minstrel
a wounded knight

a graceful flamingo
a merry butcher
a woman of means
a mindless misfit
a dreadful old woman
a soft and luscious nymph
a snarling monster

What is happening? Is your hero/heroine...

locked in a castle
under a spell
held underwater
chased by a monster
preparing to die
sitting by the fire
praying desperately
crying for help

lost in a maze in the garden
tied to the mast of a ship
happily tilling the land
saying "I do"
flying a kite
fixing the nets
driving a stake

 ~ Remember, this is a fairy tale so all manner of potions, curses, death wishes and spells help make your story richer and make a place for your emotions ~

The next part is about what you are holding onto or what is holding onto you. Make this part rich enough in detail to say what you mean but still maintain the objectivity of the reporter.

The ruthless master found all manner of diabolical...
The ugly witch always made her life miserable by...
The wretched king would forever humiliate...
The nasty sister delighted in...
The crafty thief first won her heart and then...
Suddenly the beautiful child changed into...
The old man laughed as spiked balls rained down from the heavens...
He thought the innkeeper merciful but instead she turned into...
The frog unexpectedly turned into a vicious warrior...

Then bring someone in to save the day. It could be an outsider or the heroine/hero:

> The princess/prince finally woke up...
> The spell was broken and the magical monkey...
> When this happened the...
> It was the biggest surprise to the prince/princess when ...
> The strange thing was that the gargoyle suddenly took on a ...
> She/he could stand it no more...
> It was like the years melted away and...
> Something changed and the world she/he knew would never be...
> And from the heavens descended...

The wisdom shared:

> In the bigger picture of your life...
> This was sent so you would know forever more...
> Life sends us tests and we are asked to...
> It is difficult to see why at this moment, but as your life unfolds you...
> As difficult as this has been, you will look back and understand that...
> Adversity takes us to new heights and one day you will know...

Finish with a hope-filled message for you in the here and now. Through the you, who is the storyteller, speak to the you in the present, the one who has been holding negative energy on this incident. Speak kindly and offer just one thought that will assist the you in the present, so you will feel comforted and perhaps more able to release the hold this incident has on you.

This is how it looks...

...setting the stage

This a little fable about a woman who is very angry about how isolating her upbringing was and how she felt robbed of her creative talents.

... the story

In the salt mines of Sanso in the Middle years, there lived a very lonely child. This child's name was Cumol. The reason she was so lonely was that her whole family got to work in the salt mines while she, because she was born without hands, was forced to paint pictures with her toes. It was so sad for her because her whole family laughed at her because she was different.

One day she took her pictures to the marketplace and there she met a crafty thief who first won her heart and then before she knew it she was saying 'I do" when he asked if she thought it was a good idea if he held on to things for her. He offered to hold the money she made when she sold a picture. He of course ran away with her heart, her money and her remaining pictures. _When this happened_, the lonely child said "No more. I will never love or trust again".

...wisdom from the past and a hope-filled message for the you in the present

Life sends us tests and we are asked to learn and grow from the pain we endure. Child, as you grow into adulthood - learn first to love and trust yourself. When you do, the wonders and joy of life will be yours.

My fairy tale

...setting the stage

....the story

...wisdom from the past and a hope-filled message for the you in the present

Plugging into energy from the future

If we are drained of energy by holding onto things in the past, tapping into the energy of our potential in the future can in fact energize us. One is able to do this by creating a dream. What is it that you yearn for in work? What would make it meaningful?

Remember when you were young. You used to tell people what you were going to be when you grew up. That was your dream, your heart's desire. As you grew older, chances are you forgot what you wanted 'to be'. You stopped wondering and dreaming and focused only on what you and others in your life thought you should 'do'.

Doing the work you love is like that emotional high runners get when they run. It's the sense of accomplishment when you create art, the mastery of a new culinary delight or the sense of peace that comes from meditating, fishing, building a bookshelf or doing your own special thing.

THIS WILL BE YOUR FIRST STEP IN CREATING MEANINGFUL WORK

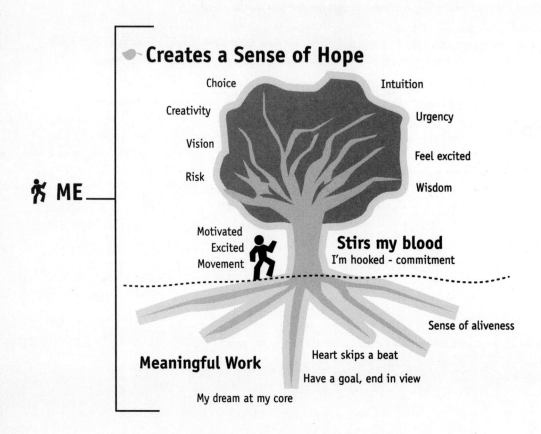

ME

Creates a Sense of Hope

Choice

Creativity

Vision

Risk

Intuition

Urgency

Feel excited

Wisdom

Motivated
Excited
Movement

Stirs my blood
I'm hooked - commitment

Sense of aliveness

Meaningful Work

Heart skips a beat

Have a goal, end in view

My dream at my core

**~ You can see how a dream is pivotal to moving forward...
the Entrepreneurial Way ~**

Dreams are not about emotion. If your dreams were only about emotion then the chances are very good that they would evaporate in the bad times, in the times when the cards are not turning up in your favor.

Dreams are at the core of your being, at the heart of the matter...some would say that dreams are of the heart. Dreams call you back and encourage you not to quit. Dreams want to be heard. Your life experience helps create a wonderful background mosaic that will ultimately help you realize your dreams.

If your heart is in something...you are following what has meaning for you as opposed to what you think you "should" do. Not everything you do will have meaning in this moment, but it is your challenge to find the thread of meaning in what you do as it relates to your greater dreams.

Discover your dream

To help you tap into the energy of the future, you would want to give yourself license to discover what in fact your dream might be. Your answer might be:

"I want a good job, excellent salary and a cottage."

Perhaps you could look at this dream statement a little differently. Would it be possible for you to move out of the left side of your brain (your intellectual) and move into the right side (your creative)?

Could you then create thoughts not about money, for money is just a method of exchange, but of what type of job you would appreciate, who you would be working with and how you would feel every morning getting up to go to that job? What would that salary make you feel like? Would the job be about that salary or would meaningful work frame the salary in a different light? And your cottage…would it be high on a mountain or by the water's edge? Would you go there alone or with whom and when you get there, what would you do? How would it make you feel? Is there any interrelationship between what you do at the cottage and what you are doing at work?

Dreams reveal what is important to you. Your dreams are about your gifts and talents. Dreams are very personal to you and thus ensure your involvement. Your dream supports you and has the ability to carry you through all the hurdles you face in your quest for meaning.

Giving shape to your dream

It will help to give your dreams shape and form if you can express your dream in another medium, one that requires you to take a risk and express in another way what you really dream for yourself.

This creative exercise can be done in any manner that appeals to your creative self, including sketch, cartoon, carving, sculpture, Lego model, music, poetry, mind mapping or any other creative form that appeals to you.

 ~ This exercise is important and it involves taking a risk. Once completed its message will help you sustain momentum, the kind of momentum you will need to propel you through this book and take you where you choose to go ~

If creative art does not appeal to you why not try some non-dominant handwriting. Remember, neatness is not a concern in this exercise…just write! Hold your pencil in the hand you would not normally write with. Start to write about your dreams and keep writing for ten minutes without raising your pencil from the paper. (Since you are tapping into a side of your brain that you don't readily access, perhaps you will get some "dream" insights that you might otherwise have missed.)

Examining your creation

Once you have created your dream you will want to examine what you have created to see what it means for you. Within the dream could be some guideposts that will give light and energy to where you wish to go.

WHAT IS THE THREAD THAT RUNS THROUGH EVERYTHING YOU'VE RECORDED?

WHAT ARE YOU PURSUING CURRENTLY THAT IS RELATED TO WHAT YOU HAVE DESCRIBED AS YOUR VISION FOR YOURSELF?

Putting words to your dream

Once you have completed this exercise, write a statement of your vision (no more than 15 words). Make it clear and direct and what you want.

IF I WERE TO EXPRESS MY DREAM IN WORDS I WOULD DESCRIBE IT AS...

Make this statement your motivator.

 ~ You could in fact call this your guiding star ~

Go back to the Circle of Choice Dynamic in *The Entrepreneurial Way*. Get a sense of where you are and what you need to do. Look at the Entrepreneurial Traits you should be focusing on at this time.

MANAGING MY PERSPECTIVE

Managing My Perspective focuses on understanding what meaningful work is for you and offers the possibility that you might find meaning in the work that you are currently doing, even though at this moment, you might feel otherwise. Working through this section, you will look at the differences between what you say about your work and what you really mean. In the process you might discover that on the surface, your work does meet many of your needs for being meaningful. You might also discover that even in the face of that logical information, you still find yourself saying how unhappy you are, how you really do dislike your job.

To help you frame what might be happening in the here and now, this section offers insights to help bring into balance your conscious and unconscious perspectives about work in general and your current work situation in particular. To do this you will have an opportunity to take a look at how you view the work you do now, have done in the past, or are planning do in the future. At the same time, you will have occasion to observe your own personal beliefs about the concept of work.

Ish wonders about the world of work

 ~ If the statistics are true, then we are quite safe in saying that there is a whole lot of unhappiness coming to work every day. Some studies have indicated that as many as 70% to 85% (or higher) of people say that they are unhappy with their work. This very high statistic does not surprise me. The workplace of the eighties and nineties engendered feelings among people in the workforce of fear, anger, distrust, anxiety and distress...and most of those feelings were never acknowledged. Just about everyone knew someone who had been affected by all the mergers, acquisitions and downsizing, so the feelings experienced were incredibly personal. The fact is, these very real feelings still exist today and for many people in today's workforce, they probably sit just below the surface. Small wonder that people do not find joy or meaning in their work.

For the individual this means - find your place! Do the career management work you need to do so you will be clear on what is meaningful for you, and where you want to go. If you have a plan for moving forward, you are much less likely to get caught in the pea soup of emotions that you no doubt encounter every day.

Managing My Perspective asks good questions! I encourage you to plumb the depths for your answers ~

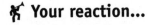 **Your reaction...**

To begin with...ask yourself these questions

HAVE YOU EVER FELT THAT YOU JUST HATED YOUR JOB?

HAVE YOU EVER BECOME SO DISILLUSIONED WITH A JOB THAT YOU JUST QUIT AND NEVER REALLY UNDERSTOOD WHAT WAS WRONG WITH THAT JOB?

HAVE YOU EVER BEEN IN A JOB THAT YOU KNEW WAS A GOOD JOB AND YOU SHOULD BE HAPPY BUT YOU JUST WEREN'T?

HAVE YOU EVER FACED A DECISION TO ACCEPT A JOB OFFER BUT YOU KNEW OR FELT THAT SOMETHING WASN'T RIGHT?

HAVE YOU EVER ACCEPTED A JOB THAT WAS SIMILAR TO A PRIOR JOB THAT WAS UNSATISFACTORY, BUT EVERYTHING SEEMED TO TURN AROUND FOR THE BETTER IN THE NEW JOB?

HAVE YOU EVER FACED THE DECISION OF CHOOSING BETWEEN TWO JOB OFFERS THAT FELT QUITE DIFFERENT IN NATURE AND YET EACH APPEARED ON THE SURFACE TO OFFER SIMILAR CHALLENGES AND REWARDS? WHY DO YOU THINK THAT WAS SO?

My current perspective

Record your perspective about your current work situation. The more specific and open you can be about your current perspective, the clearer your insights will be as you work through this section.

IN THE BIG PICTURE, MY CURRENT JOB IS...

THE THINGS THAT I FIND VERY GRATIFYING ARE...

THERE ARE SOME ASPECTS, SITUATIONS, PEOPLE AND POLICIES THAT CAUSE...

GENERALLY MY CURRENT PERSPECTIVE IS...

Your current perspective, whether positive or negative or a bit of both is real and is influencing you. Keep this in mind as you proceed through the upcoming exercises and record any of your reactions or insights.

The following exercise is designed to help you explore different aspects of your past or present work experiences or your future work experiences that you are currently considering. This exercise will help you to identify what is meaningful or important to you in your work life, as you examine different aspects of your work.

Meaningful Work Indicators Assessment

The following worksheet lists 20 different aspects of work. Review these different aspects of work to familiarize yourself with them. Complete each step in the exercise before going on to the next.

 ~ As you work through this exercise, go with your first instinct in responding ~

STEP 1

In the **Check** column, check off ten aspects from the **Aspect** list that have the most meaning or relevance to you and your needs in a work environment. This exercise will focus only on those ten chosen aspects.

STEP 2

Examine closely the ten aspects you have chosen. In the **Rank** column, rank them 10 through 1...with 10 the "Most Important" to 1 "Least Important". When you finish you should have ten items rank ordered from 10 to 1 in the **Rank** column.

Sometimes it's easier to rank the most important (10) then the least important (1), then 9 then 2.

STEP 3

Pick two or three jobs that you want to evaluate. You can choose from:
- previous work experiences in different companies
- previous and current positions within a company
- a position you have applied for
- a position that you are researching as a possible career move
- a well-defined volunteer position

In the Positions (marked 1, 2, 3) identify the two or three jobs that you have chosen to evaluate (e.g. sales clerk, office manager, driver, vice president, executive director).

STEP 4

Examine each Position that you listed. Only consider the 10 aspects that you checked off. Give yourself a mark from 1 (being low) to 10 (being high), using the following question:

"In this position, to what degree was this particular aspect: achieved, satisfied, realized, provided, accomplished." (Use the phrase that applies for you.) Place this mark in the Score column.

 ~ This exercise will be more insightful if you evaluate one job completely, then the second, then the third ~

STEP 5

Multiply each Score number by the corresponding Rank number in the left column. Place the answer in the adjacent Total column. Once you have Step 4 completed for all ten aspects add up the Total column. Place that number in the Sum box at the bottom of the page.

MEANINGFUL WORK INDICATORS ASSESSMENT

			POSITION 1		POSITION 2		POSITION 3	
Check	Rank	Aspect	Score	Total	Score	Total	Score	Total
☐	☐	Necessary materials and equipment for my job						
☐	☐	Opportunity to do what I do best						
☐	☐	Work independently and set own goals						
☐	☐	Clearly defined duties and tasks						
☐	☐	Consideration of work/life balance issues						
☐	☐	Opportunity to learn and grow						
☐	☐	Sense of contribution to company's mission						
☐	☐	An outlet to express creative initiative						
☐	☐	Ethical work environment						
☐	☐	Sense of meaning or purpose						
☐	☐	Open communication, feedback and teamwork						
☐	☐	Coworkers committed to quality work						
☐	☐	Sense that my opinion counts						
☐	☐	Praise and recognition of my contribution often						
☐	☐	Sense of community/camaraderie at work						
☐	☐	Achieve financial needs						
☐	☐	Adequate perks/benefits/remuneration						
☐	☐	Training and development encouraged						
☐	☐	Reasonable job security						
☐	☐	Results/productivity						
				SUM		SUM		SUM

What you have completed is a grid that can be used to look at your work experiences from different perspectives so you can see what was/is really important to you. You will be able to step back and objectively assess why some jobs have seemed "a better fit" for you and your skills and abilities.

At first glance!

This is a general guideline for you to assess your feelings about a past, current or future job:

What your score suggests

0 - 200 **Not a happy place...consider changing.**
It seems that so many important aspects are not in place for you. You might want to ask, "What am I really getting from this position?"

200 - 250 **Position is OK...but you should be open to change.**
Some aspects are OK but there are a few that are just not right. Perhaps you should be keeping your options open.

250 - 300 **Very acceptable position...there's something meaningful here for you.**
Very important aspects are being provided although some areas could use improvement. Proactively examine what you can change!

300+ **Very satisfying...sense of achievement in priority aspects.**
You have many important aspects being achieved and the job is meaningful to you!

Upon further thought!

You may discover that how you scored different **Positions** was influenced by the fact that several very important aspects were not being provided. Or the opposite was true a few important aspects were provided but several less important aspects were not in place. What matters here is: what was the combination that worked best for you?

Look back at the **Positions** you selected and examine them in three groups based on their **Rank**:

- your top ranked aspects 10 through 8
- your next important aspects 7 through 5
- your remaining aspects 4 through 1

Can you identify what was different between **Positions**? Perhaps you can focus on specific situations in different jobs to clearly identify what might have been at the core of your frustration or elation in a particular work setting. This will help you identify and clearly state what is important for you in a work environment.

There was a teacher. When she finally sought advice, all she could focus on was how much she hated her job. After months of soul-searching, she decided to take a leave of absence. Three months later she discovered, to her surprise, that it was not the job she hated but the stress and anxiety she experienced in the job. Identifying and dealing with her stress issues allowed her to return to her teaching position.

An individual with a professional designation was working on her articles at a very big firm…a job sought after by many. Eleven months later she quit her job. She absolutely hated it. Upon closer scrutiny, she discovered that what was missing in that job, which had been present in others that she had held, was a sense of closeness among coworkers. Moving to a smaller firm made all the difference. Consider that although all other things were equal, it was a need for community that made the difference.

A professional had been very successfully employed through the first fifteen years of his career. He found himself in a job that made him terribly unhappy, unhappy to the point that he decided he had to quit. As he examined his reasons in retrospect, he realized that much of his problem was centered on the kind of person he was and his own personal aspirations. He did not enjoy working with an organization that was autocratic and did not encourage creativity. Through a self-assessment process he examined what his key motivators were. Knowing what for him was essential in the environment and the management style of a potential employer helped him prepare far more effectively for interviews.

Your significant Work-Life moments...

An "on the surface" perspective

The twenty aspects in the Meaningful Work Indicators worksheet were listed in clusters of five statements and are divisible into four specific groups.
Take another look at where you clustered your priorities; were your choices clustered around a certain group of aspects?

Work Environment

Necessary materials and equipment for my job
Opportunity to do what I do best
Work independently and set own goals
Clearly defined duties and tasks
Consideration of work/life balance issues

*How many did you pick?*_____

Interpersonal

Open communication, feedback and teamwork
Coworkers committed to quality work
Sense that my opinion counts
Praise and recognition of my contribution often
Sense of community/camaraderie at work

*How many did you pick?*_____

Values

Opportunity to learn and grow
Sense of contribution to company's mission
An outlet to express creative initiative
Ethical work environment
Sense of meaning or purpose

*How many did you pick?*_____

Tangible

Achieve financial needs
Adequate perks/benefits/remuneration
Training and development encouraged
Reasonable job security
Results/productivity

*How many did you pick?*_____

FROM THIS EXERCISE WHAT DO YOU CONCLUDE IS IMPORTANT TO YOU IN YOUR PURSUIT OF MEANINGFUL WORK?

HAS THIS INFORMATION CAST NEW LIGHT ON HOW YOU EXPRESSED YOUR CURRENT PERSPECTIVE? (SEE MY CURRENT PERSPECTIVE EXERCISE ON PAGE 85.)

IS THERE SOME ASPECT THAT YOU NOW REALIZE IS VERY IMPORTANT TO YOU THAT WAS NOT INCLUDED IN THE MEANINGFUL WORK INDICATORS ASSESSMENT? PLEASE MAKE NOTE OF THAT ASPECT BECAUSE IT IS OBVIOUSLY VERY IMPORTANT TO YOU.

An "underlying" perspective

What we say to ourselves and/or to others and "the message behind the message" are often different. You will see that the following exchange between Person A and Person B comes from two entirely different places. You might think of the first as being the intellectual intent of the interaction and the second, as being the emotional intent.

This picture shows the exchange one way:

Person A	Person B
I hate this job!	You've got that right... There's incompetents running this place.
INTELLECTUAL INTENT	
EMOTIONAL INTENT	
I hate being unsure of my Future. I'm afraid.	What if they can't save the place? I don't trust them.

HEAD

HEART

Often it is difficult to be clear on what motivates and influences us. We no doubt believe we are quite aware of our conscious mind and so feel quite comfortable with decisions made at that level. What we are less comfortable with or perhaps unaware of is our unconscious mind. We are less clear how our unconscious influences us at a conscious level nor do we have a clear sense how that plays out in our thinking, our acting and our doing.

This alone, the fact that we are not always aware of what is making us feel like we feel, can have a considerable impact on our interpretation of what we are really feeling about work.

Getting right down to it

The **Meaningful Work Indicators** exercise helped you understand what you think about your work…let's say you discovered that you ranked your current position at a rather high level. However, on the first page of this section you also identified your **Current Perspective**. Let's say you identified quite emphatically that you were fed up…that you were not pleased with your job. This doesn't mean you were lying to yourself, or that there is a right or wrong about how it turned out for you. What it does mean is that any one of us can have many things churning around inside us at any given time and different stimuli will bring different things to the surface.

This exercise should be helpful to give clarity to your results. Examine your intellectual conclusions regarding the **Meaningful Work Indicators Assessment** and your **Current Perspective**. Once completed, then dig a little deeper. What do you really mean at an emotional level?

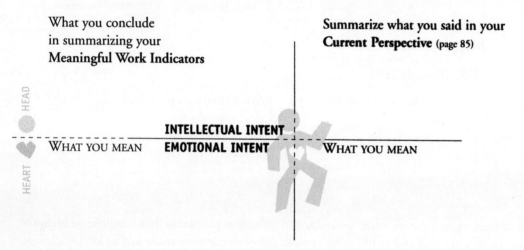

What you conclude in summarizing your **Meaningful Work Indicators**

Summarize what you said in your **Current Perspective** (page 85)

HEAD

HEART

INTELLECTUAL INTENT

WHAT YOU MEAN   EMOTIONAL INTENT   WHAT YOU MEAN

DO YOU SEE CONSISTENCY BETWEEN YOUR THOUGHTS AND YOUR FEELINGS?

DO YOU SEE GREAT DISCREPANCY BETWEEN WHAT YOU SAY AND WHAT YOU MEAN?

Step back a moment...

This exercise will give you additional insights into what work means to you. The questions are meant to assist you in a self-remembering and self-observing process.

How did you see work when you were a child? Did you look forward to the day when you could work? Why?

What did you learn from your family of origin about work? Was it a necessary evil, a great source of failure, an expression of accomplishment...what?

When you were young, what did you imagine you would be doing when you were the age you are now?

What are your siblings' views about work? Are they similar to yours or very different?

If different from yours, do you have any insights why they would be different?

Do you feel competitive with one or all of your siblings about what you've accomplished in your career? Why? How did that competition get started?

In your family of origin was meaningful work a consideration?

What are you teaching your children about work?

Once you have answered these questions, sit with them for a while. You might find that these questions could bring you great insights about some of your views about work that are affecting how you feel today. This exercise asks you to take another look at your current position and overall situation in your workplace and asks you to consider your options.

"Better than" option

In the light of the exercises I have just completed in *Managing My Perspective*, I realize that the position I now hold is a better fit for me than I originally thought.

IF CHANGE IS NEEDED TO MAKE THIS JOB EVEN BETTER, IS THERE SOMETHING I CAN DO TO FACILITATE THAT CHANGE?

WILL THAT CHANGE COME FROM WITHIN ME, FROM MY MINDSET, MY ATTITUDE OR MY BELIEFS? HOW?

WHO ULTIMATELY, OTHER THAN MYSELF, CAN MAKE CHANGES THAT CAN MAKE THIS JOB BETTER FOR ME?

WHAT WOULD BE AN IMPARTIAL INDIVIDUAL'S PERSPECTIVE OF MY JOB?

WHAT DO I NEED TO KNOW ABOUT WHAT IS REALLY TRUE IN THIS SITUATION AND WHO WILL TELL ME?

WHAT WOULD BE THE ACID TEST TO ASSESS WHETHER MY PERSPECTIVE IS VALID?

TO WHAT DEGREE IS MY SENSE OF JOB SATISFACTION BASED ON MY ORIGINAL PERSPECTIVE?

"Time for a change" option

AFTER COMPLETING THESE EXERCISES AM I OF THE OPINION THAT THERE IS NOTHING SALVAGEABLE OR REDEEMABLE ABOUT MY POSITION?

HAVE I ANSWERED ALL THE QUESTIONS IN THE "BETTER THAN" OPTION FULLY?

DID I FIND A CREDIBLE THIRD PARTY TO ASSIST ME IN VALIDATING MY DECISION?

HAVE I DISCUSSED THIS FULLY WITH MY PARTNER? DO I HAVE THEIR SUPPORT? IF NO, WHAT CAN I DO THAT WILL HELP THEM COME TO THE POINT OF BEING SUPPORTIVE?

AS IT IS MUCH EASIER TO GET A NEW JOB WHEN I HAVE A JOB - WHAT PLAN WILL I PUT IN PLACE TO FACILITATE MY TRANSITION?

WHAT TIME LINE WILL I SET FOR MYSELF, SO I HAVE A BUILT-IN MECHANISM FOR MOVING FORWARD? HOW WILL I MAINTAIN MOMENTUM?

Making informed decisions!

Making choices isn't necessarily about always making RIGHT or WRONG decisions. Rather, you might want to look at it as a process of doing good research, understanding your options and making INFORMED decisions.

Go back to the Circle of Choice Dynamic and see where you are, what you need and what entrepreneurial traits will best serve you at this time. Remember that just thinking about what you have discovered here in these exercises is only thinking. You could easily sit on those thoughts for years, never choosing, just waiting, until the circumstances of your life make the choice for you. Don't wait! Find the energy to make something happen...now!

6

MANAGING MY DEVELOPMENT

Core attributes self-assessment

The objective of this exercise is to facilitate a process to help you clearly assess your strengths and natural abilities and to pinpoint areas of potential yet to be realized. It should offer good insight into where you can focus future efforts in your personal development.

As well, it is about taking a fair look at you. If in your objective assessment you register a lower score in some areas, well, that says you are prepared to be honest with yourself...but not brutal. This is after all a Career Management continuum, so you can hardly be expected to know it all ever. There is always room for new knowledge - it is a sign that you are alive and growing.

 ~ Know that it is easy to make observations and intellectual choices...but the real growth comes in putting a decision you've made into motion ~

In each section you will be asked to assess two key factors regarding these seven core attributes:

- 🏃 COMMUNICATE
- 🏃 THINK
- 🏃 LEARN
- 🏃 POSITIVE ATTITUDE AND BEHAVIOR
- 🏃 RESPONSIBILITY
- 🏃 ADAPTABILITY
- 🏃 TEAMWORK

Ability

For each aspect of each of these core attributes, you will be asked whether "I am able to..." do something. As you answer, consider how the presence or absence of this aspect has aided or deterred you in your Work-Life. Do you think not having it could seriously affect your future career moves or, conversely, does having it give you a platform to move to another level?

Applicability

Are you effective in how you apply each attribute in your Work-Life? Do you approach personal and work life differently? If you do, have you thought that some work aspects in which you have proficiency could be transferred to your personal life (and vice versa)? This section will help you identify to what degree you can say "I have effectively applied this in the following circumstances..."

At the end of each section, you will be asked to bring all your scores forward. These scores will give you a clear picture of your current strengths and good directional information about the focus of your personal and professional development. This will then provide the framework for a **Personal Development Action Plan**...the natural conclusion to this exercise.

COMMUNICATE

I know how to speak clearly, and how to explain my ideas to others, one-on-one and in groups.

DESCRIBE A TIME WHEN YOU SPOKE CLEARLY AND SUCCESSFULLY EXPLAINED YOUR IDEAS.

HOW OFTEN DO YOU HAVE THE OPPORTUNITY TO APPLY THESE SKILLS? BE SPECIFIC!

IN THIS SITUATION, IDENTIFY HOW YOU FELT AS YOU WERE DOING THIS. (BE SPECIFIC: I ENJOYED...I WAS TERRIFIED...)

GIVEN THE CHANCE, DO YOU AVOID THE OPPORTUNITY TO PRACTICE THESE SKILLS?

DO YOU KNOW NOW WHY YOU FELT THAT WAY? (WELL-PREPARED, NOT REHEARSED...)

DO YOU SEEK OUT OPPORTUNITIES TO PRACTICE AND IMPROVE YOUR SKILLS?

HOW DO YOU KNOW YOU HAVE EFFECTIVELY COMMUNICATED YOUR IDEAS?

Now rate yourself...be fair, be kind and be honest. Consider your personal life and how it is affected by this attribute. Note *Your Thoughts*...in the space provided at the end of this book.

A. ABILITY
How well is this attribute developed?

| 1 WEAK | 2 | 3 | 4 | 5 STRONG |

B. APPLICABILITY
How often do I really demonstrate it?

| 1 WEAK | 2 | 3 | 4 | 5 STRONG |

MY SCORE
(A X B)

(=)

COMMUNICATE

I listen to, understand and learn from others.

WHAT QUALITIES DO YOU HAVE THAT MAKE YOU AN EFFECTIVE LISTENER?

HOW DO YOU PERFORM THESE SKILLS DIFFERENTLY IN PROFESSIONAL, PERSONAL, VOLUNTEER OR WORK-RELATED SITUATIONS?

HAVE PEOPLE EVER COMMENTED ON YOUR LISTENING ABILITIES? POSITIVELY OR NEGATIVELY?

WHAT MEANS DO YOU USE TO ENSURE YOU UNDERSTAND WHAT IS BEING SAID?

ARE THERE DIFFERENCES IN YOUR EFFECTIVENESS WHEN COMMUNICATING IN PERSON OR BY PHONE?

WHAT IS YOUR MEANS OF ASSESSING WHETHER YOU HAVE LEARNED FROM ANOTHER PERSON?

HOW DO YOU DISCERN WHEN ANOTHER PERSON HAS SOMETHING TO TEACH YOU?

Now rate yourself…be fair, be kind and be honest. Consider your personal life and how it is affected by this attribute. Note *Your Thoughts*…in the space provided at the end of this book.

A. ABILITY
How well is this attribute developed?

1 WEAK	2	3	4	5 STRONG

B. APPLICABILITY
How often do I really demonstrate it?

1 WEAK	2	3	4	5 STRONG

MY SCORE
(A X B)

(=)

COMMUNICATE

I am able to write letters and reports that are clearly understood.

HOW DO YOU ORGANIZE YOUR THOUGHTS BEFORE YOU WRITE?

DO YOU HAVE STANDARD FORMATS AND RULES FOR EFFECTIVE WRITING? EXAMPLE: IF YOU ARE ASKED TO WRITE A THREE-PAGE REPORT, WHAT DO YOU DO?

DESCRIBE A TIME WHEN YOUR WRITTEN COMMUNICATION WAS MISUNDERSTOOD.

HOW OFTEN DO YOU HAVE OCCASION TO PRACTICE THESE SKILLS?

WHAT DID YOU LEARN FROM THIS EXPERIENCE?

WHAT MAKES YOU SO SURE YOUR LETTERS AND REPORTS ARE CLEARLY UNDERSTOOD?

Now rate yourself...be fair, be kind and be honest. Consider your personal life and how it is affected by this attribute. Note *Your Thoughts...*in the space provided at the end of this book.

A. ABILITY
How well is this attribute developed?

| 1 WEAK | 2 | 3 | 4 | 5 STRONG |

B. APPLICABILITY
How often do I really demonstrate it?

| 1 WEAK | 2 | 3 | 4 | 5 STRONG |

MY SCORE
(A X B)

=

COMMUNICATE

I am able to read and interpret written instructions, correspondence or graphic materials well.

DESCRIBE AN OCCASION WHEN YOU SUCCESSFULLY INTERPRETED INSTRUCTIONS THAT OTHERS WERE NOT ABLE TO UNDERSTAND.	WHAT KINDS OF WRITTEN INSTRUCTIONS, CORRESPONDENCE OR GRAPHIC MATERIALS ARE YOU NORMALLY ASKED TO READ AND INTERPRET?
WHAT SKILL DO YOU HAVE THAT ALLOWED YOU TO DO THIS WHEN OTHERS COULD NOT?	WHEN WAS THE LAST TIME YOU WERE GIVEN VERY CHALLENGING INFORMATION TO READ AND INTERPRET?
HOW DO YOU PRACTICE THIS SKILL?	IF YOU ARE NOT BEING GIVEN THAT BY OTHERS, WHAT ARE YOU DOING TO CHALLENGE YOURSELF?

Now rate yourself...be fair, be kind and be honest. Consider your personal life and how it is affected by this attribute. Note *Your Thoughts...*in the space provided at the end of this book.

A. ABILITY
How well is this attribute developed?

1 WEAK	2	3	4	5 STRONG

B. APPLICABILITY
How often do I really demonstrate it?

1 WEAK	2	3	4	5 STRONG

MY SCORE
(A X B)

(=)

COMMUNICATE

I am able to 'read between the lines', observing others through their body language, voice, energy level and other non-verbal cues.

DESCRIBE AN OCCASION WHEN YOU FIGURED OUT WHAT WAS HAPPENING BEFORE ANYONE SAID ANYTHING.

WOULD YOU ESTIMATE THAT YOU READ BETWEEN THE LINES TWO OR THREE TIMES A DAY?

WHAT WOULD BE THE MAJOR WAYS THAT OBSERVERS READ BETWEEN YOUR LINES? WHAT NON-VERBAL COMMUNICATION CUES TEND TO INDICATE WHAT YOU ARE THINKING?

WHAT CRITERIA DO YOU USE TO MEASURE BODY LANGUAGE, VOICE, ENERGY LEVEL, ETC. IN OTHERS?

WHAT SIGNS DO YOU WATCH FOR IN HELPING YOU UNDERSTAND WHAT IS GOING ON BEHIND ANOTHER'S WORDS?

HOW WELL DO YOU MEASURE UP IN THESE CATEGORIES?

HOW WELL WOULD YOU MEASURE UP TO YOUR OWN CRITERIA?

Now rate yourself…be fair, be kind and be honest. Consider your personal life and how it is affected by this attribute. Note *Your Thoughts…*in the space provided at the end of this book.

A. ABILITY
How well is this attribute developed?

1 WEAK	2	3	4	5 STRONG

B. APPLICABILITY
How often do I really demonstrate it?

1 WEAK	2	3	4	5 STRONG

MY SCORE
(A X B)

=

MANAGING MY DEVELOPMENT... CHAPTER 6

Summary Assessment

COMMUNICATE

Now that you have examined the five key components of the Core Attribute Communicate, it is time to draw some personal conclusions.

STRENGTH:

WHAT HAVE YOU DISCOVERED ABOUT YOURSELF THAT YOU WOULD IDENTIFY AS THE STRONGEST CHARACTERISTIC YOU HAVE REGARDING COMMUNICATION?

Identify areas in your personal or professional life where the strengths that you identified in your Communicate core attributes profile could be used as a self-empowering quality that can help further your career or enrich your life.

CHALLENGE:

WHAT COMPONENTS OF COMMUNICATION HAVE YOU IDENTIFIED AS AREAS THAT YOU SHOULD DEVELOP, TO HELP YOU RIGHT NOW? WHAT ACTION WILL YOU CHOOSE TO MAKE THIS HAPPEN?

WHAT ASPECT OF COMMUNICATION HAVE YOU IDENTIFIED AS AN AREA THAT YOU SHOULD IMPROVE UPON TO HELP YOU IN THE FUTURE? WHAT ACTION SHOULD YOU TAKE AND WHEN?

Overall Score

For your *Communicate* Assessment Summary, bring forward your individual scores and place them in the appropriate box below. This score will be used later in the chapter, to help you create an action plan for your future.

	I know how to speak clearly, and to explain my ideas to others, one-on-one and in groups.
	I listen to, understand and learn from others.
	I am able to write letters and reports that are clearly understood.
	I am able to read and interpret written instructions, correspondence or graphic materials well.
	I am able to "read between the lines", observing others through their body language, voice, energy level and other non-verbal cues.

	MY TOTAL SCORE:

THINK

I think critically and evaluate problems before making decisions.

How would you define critical thinking?

What was a major personal decision you dealt with recently?

Identify a specific situation where you demonstrated critical thinking.

Were you effective in implementing your solutions?

In that situation did you make definitive decisions or did you second-guess yourself?

What was the last significant work-related problem that you had to resolve?

How do you know you were effective in dealing with it?

Now rate yourself...be fair, be kind and be honest. Consider your personal life and how it is affected by this attribute. Note *Your Thoughts*...in the space provided at the end of this book.

A. ABILITY
How well is this attribute developed?

| 1 WEAK | 2 | 3 | 4 | 5 STRONG |

B. APPLICABILITY
How often do I really demonstrate it?

| 1 WEAK | 2 | 3 | 4 | 5 STRONG |

MY SCORE
(A X B)

=

THINK

I understand and can solve problems involving basic mathematics.

HOW EFFECTIVELY DID YOU APPLY YOURSELF
TO MATHEMATICAL ACADEMIC STUDIES?

HOW ACCURATE ARE YOU?

HOW DO YOU APPLY BASIC MATH SKILLS ON
A REGULAR BASIS?

WHAT METHOD DO YOU USE TO MEASURE
YOUR ACCURACY?

Now rate yourself...be fair, be kind and be honest. Consider your personal life and how it is affected by this attribute. Note *Your Thoughts*...in the space provided at the end of this book.

A. ABILITY
How well is this attribute developed?

1	2	3	4	5
WEAK				STRONG

B. APPLICABILITY
How often do I really demonstrate it?

1	2	3	4	5
WEAK				STRONG

MY SCORE
(A X B)

=

THINK

I can use technology, instruments, tools and information systems effectively.

HOW CURRENT ARE YOU WITH NEW TECHNOLOGY OR SYSTEMS IN YOUR FIELD OF WORK OR INTEREST?

DO YOU USE NEW TECHNOLOGY/INSTRUMENTS THE SAME WAY EVERY DAY OR DO YOU CHALLENGE YOURSELF TO BE CREATIVE? HOW?

HOW WOULD YOU DESCRIBE YOUR CURRENT LEVEL OF WORKING KNOWLEDGE OF COMPUTERS AND BASIC SOFTWARE?

HOW WOULD YOU ASSESS YOUR KNOWLEDGE COMPARED TO OTHERS IN SIMILAR POSITIONS?

WHAT HAVE YOU DONE TO MAINTAIN OR UPGRADE YOUR SKILLS OVER THE PAST ONE TO THREE YEARS?

WHEN YOU DON'T UNDERSTAND NEW TECHNOLOGY/INSTRUMENTS, WHAT DO YOU DO ABOUT IT?

HOW DO YOU KEEP AWARE OF NEW DEVELOPMENTS THAT WILL HAVE TO BE LEARNED/APPLIED?

Now rate yourself…be fair, be kind and be honest. Consider your personal life and how it is affected by this attribute. Note *Your Thoughts…*in the space provided at the end of this book.

A. ABILITY
How well is this attribute developed?

1 WEAK	2	3	4	5 STRONG

B. APPLICABILITY
How often do I really demonstrate it?

1 WEAK	2	3	4	5 STRONG

MY SCORE
(A X B)

(=)

THINK

I can reason well and make objective judgments.

IDENTIFY A SITUATION WHEN SOMEONE CAME TO YOU FOR OBJECTIVE ADVICE PERSONALLY OR PROFESSIONALLY.

HOW DO YOU MAINTAIN OBJECTIVITY IN YOUR DECISION-MAKING?

HOW WOULD YOU EVALUATE HOW YOU HANDLED THE SITUATION?

DESCRIBE THE REASONING PROCESS YOU USE IN MAKING OBJECTIVE DECISIONS.

Now rate yourself…be fair, be kind and be honest. Consider your personal life and how it is affected by this attribute. Note *Your Thoughts*…in the space provided at the end of this book.

A. ABILITY
How well is this attribute developed?

| 1 WEAK | 2 | 3 | 4 | 5 STRONG |

B. APPLICABILITY
How often do I really demonstrate it?

| 1 WEAK | 2 | 3 | 4 | 5 STRONG |

MY SCORE
(A X B)

(=)

THINK

I can think intuitively and evaluate risk.

GIVE AN EXAMPLE WHEN YOU FOLLOWED YOUR INTUITION.

HOW DO YOU EVALUATE THE RISKS AND CONSEQUENCES OF THE ACTIONS YOU TAKE?

WHAT WAS THE OUTCOME?

WHY WOULD AN EMPLOYER WANT YOU TO USE THESE SKILLS?

DID YOU FOLLOW YOUR INTUITION OR JUST PLAY IT SAFE?

IDENTIFY A SITUATION WHERE YOU APPLIED THESE SKILLS.

HOW DID YOU EVALUATE THE RISK INVOLVED WITH FUNCTIONING INTUITIVELY?

HOW DO YOU KNOW YOUR INTUITION IS WORKING FOR YOU?

Now rate yourself...be fair, be kind and be honest. Consider your personal life and how it is affected by this attribute. Note *Your Thoughts*...in the space provided at the end of this book.

A. ABILITY
How well is this attribute developed?

| 1 WEAK | 2 | 3 | 4 | 5 STRONG |

B. APPLICABILITY
How often do I really demonstrate it?

| 1 WEAK | 2 | 3 | 4 | 5 STRONG |

MY SCORE
(A X B)

(=)

Summary Assessment

THINK

Now that you have examined the five key components of the Core Attribute Think, it is time to draw some personal conclusions.

STRENGTH:

WHAT HAVE YOU DISCOVERED ABOUT YOURSELF THAT YOU WOULD IDENTIFY AS THE STRONGEST CHARACTERISTIC YOU HAVE REGARDING THINKING?

Identify areas in your personal or professional life where the strengths that you identified in your Think core attributes profile could be used as a self-empowering quality that can help further your career or enrich your life.

CHALLENGE:

WHAT COMPONENTS OF THINKING HAVE YOU IDENTIFIED AS AREAS THAT YOU SHOULD DEVELOP, TO HELP YOU RIGHT NOW? WHAT ACTION WILL YOU CHOOSE TO MAKE THIS HAPPEN?

WHAT ASPECT OF THINKING HAVE YOU IDENTIFIED AS AN AREA THAT YOU SHOULD IMPROVE UPON TO HELP YOU IN THE FUTURE? WHAT ACTION SHOULD YOU TAKE AND WHEN?

Overall Score

For your *Think* Assessment Summary, bring forward your individual scores and place them in the appropriate box below. This score will be used later in the chapter, to help you create an action plan for your future.

	I think critically and evaluate problems before making decisions.
	I understand and can solve problems involving basic mathematics.
	I can use technology, instruments, tools and information systems effectively.
	I can reason well and make objective judgments.
	I can think intuitively and evaluate risk.

	MY TOTAL SCORE:

LEARN

I enjoy learning and proactively continue to learn.

WHY WOULD YOU DESCRIBE YOURSELF AS A PERSON WHO ENJOYS LEARNING?

DESCRIBE FOUR OCCASIONS WHEN YOU PROACTIVELY PUT YOURSELF INTO A NEW LEARNING SITUATION.

IS HOW MUCH YOU ENJOY LEARNING CONTINGENT UPON WHO IS DOING THE TEACHING AND/OR HOW THE TEACHING IS BEING DONE?

ON WHAT BASIS DID YOU SELECT THESE NEW LEARNING OPPORTUNITIES?

WHAT HAPPENS WHEN YOU ARE CHALLENGED TO LEARN INFORMATION THAT IS NOT IN YOUR AREA OF PREFERENCE?

HOW WOULD SOMEONE WHO KNOWS YOU WELL, DESCRIBE YOUR INTEREST IN PROACTIVE CONTINUOUS LEARNING?

WHAT PROACTIVE STEPS HAVE YOU TAKEN IN THE LAST YEAR THAT WOULD INDICATE YOUR DESIRE TO LEARN CONTINUOUSLY?

Now rate yourself…be fair, be kind and be honest. Consider your personal life and how it is affected by this attribute. Note *Your Thoughts*…in the space provided at the end of this book.

A. ABILITY
How well is this attribute developed?

| 1 WEAK | 2 | 3 | 4 | 5 STRONG |

B. APPLICABILITY
How often do I really demonstrate it?

| 1 WEAK | 2 | 3 | 4 | 5 STRONG |

MY SCORE
(A X B)

(=)

LEARN

I am interested in people and events.

DESCRIBE HOW "BEING INTERESTED" IN PEOPLE AND EVENTS PLAYS OUT IN YOUR LIFE, AND WHAT IS IT THAT INTERESTS YOU?

HOW WOULD YOU DESCRIBE YOUR COMFORT ZONE IN TAKING THE INITIATIVE TO MEET NEW PEOPLE?

THROUGH WHAT MEDIUMS DO YOU TRACK EVENTS AND WHAT EVENTS ARE YOU MOST LIKELY TO TRACK?

HOW OFTEN DO YOU TAKE THE INITIATIVE TO MEET NEW PEOPLE?

HOW DO YOU RETAIN THE INFORMATION YOU GATHER AND FOR WHAT PURPOSE DO YOU RETAIN IT?

DO YOU INVOLVE YOURSELF IN DISCUSSIONS ON CURRENT EVENTS?

Now rate yourself...be fair, be kind and be honest. Consider your personal life and how it is affected by this attribute. Note *Your Thoughts...*in the space provided at the end of this book.

A. ABILITY
How well is this attribute developed?

1	2	3	4	5
WEAK				STRONG

B. APPLICABILITY
How often do I really demonstrate it?

1	2	3	4	5
WEAK				STRONG

MY SCORE
(A X B)

(=)

LEARN

I know how to read and find information when I need it.

DESCRIBE THE TYPES OF READING YOU DO.

WHEN WOULD YOU BE THE PERSON OTHERS WOULD TURN TO AS AN INFORMATION RESOURCE?

DESCRIBE HOW YOU LEARN BY SEEKING OUT MENTORING AND NETWORKING OPPORTUNITIES, I.E. LEARNING FROM OTHERS TO HELP YOU MAKE YOUR DECISIONS.

HOW DO YOU MAKE USE OF WHAT YOU READ?

DESCRIBE HOW YOU KNOW HOW TO DO YOUR OWN RESEARCH, FIND YOUR OWN INFORMATION AND MAKE YOUR OWN DECISIONS.

IT IS ESTIMATED THAT A VERY HIGH PERCENTAGE OF NORTH AMERICANS READ AT LESS THAN A GRADE 8 READING LEVEL. WHAT DOES THIS MEAN TO YOU?

Now rate yourself…be fair, be kind and be honest. Consider your personal life and how it is affected by this attribute. Note *Your Thoughts…*in the space provided at the end of this book.

A. ABILITY
How well is this attribute developed?

1	2	3	4	5
WEAK				STRONG

B. APPLICABILITY
How often do I really demonstrate it?

1	2	3	4	5
WEAK				STRONG

MY SCORE
(A X B)

LEARN

I pay attention to societal and work trends that are impacting the future now.

WHAT METHODS DO YOU USE TO IDENTIFY PERTINENT TRENDS?

WHEN YOU DO IDENTIFY A PERTINENT TREND, WHAT DO YOU DO WITH THAT INFORMATION?

WHAT DO YOU IDENTIFY AS THE TWO KEY SOCIETAL AND WORK TRENDS THAT ARE AFFECTING THE FUTURE NOW?

HAVE YOU INITIATED ANY WORK-RELATED DECISIONS BASED ON THIS INFORMATION?

HOW DO YOU JUDGE WHETHER A SOCIETAL OR WORK TREND MIGHT IMPACT YOUR FUTURE?

HOW DO YOU KEEP TRACK OF TRENDS THAT ARE MEANINGFUL TO YOU?

Now rate yourself...be fair, be kind and be honest. Consider your personal life and how it is affected by this attribute. Note *Your Thoughts*...in the space provided at the end of this book.

A. ABILITY
How well is this attribute developed?

1 WEAK	2	3	4	5 STRONG

B. APPLICABILITY
How often do I really demonstrate it?

1 WEAK	2	3	4	5 STRONG

MY SCORE
(A X B)

(=)

LEARN

I know how to filter through essential and non-essential information.

WHAT FILTERING TOOLS OR METHODS OF DISCERNMENT DO YOU USE, TO ASSESS WHETHER INFORMATION IS ESSENTIAL OR NON-ESSENTIAL?

HOW OFTEN DO YOU GET A CHANCE TO USE YOUR FILTERING SKILLS AND IN WHAT KINDS OF SITUATIONS?

HOW DO YOU REACT TO MUNDANE, REPETITIVE, GOSSIPY CONVERSATIONS?

WHY DO YOU THINK AN EMPLOYER WOULD CONSIDER THIS AN ESSENTIAL CORE SKILL?

IN WHAT CIRCUMSTANCE HAVE YOU INITIATED, PARTICIPATED IN OR AVOIDED THESE TYPES OF CONVERSATIONS?

Now rate yourself…be fair, be kind and be honest. Consider your personal life and how it is affected by this attribute. Note *Your Thoughts*…in the space provided at the end of this book.

A. ABILITY
How well is this attribute developed?

| 1 WEAK | 2 | 3 | 4 | 5 STRONG |

B. APPLICABILITY
How often do I really demonstrate it?

| 1 WEAK | 2 | 3 | 4 | 5 STRONG |

MY SCORE
(A X B)

 =

Summary Assessment

LEARN

Now that you have examined the five key components of the Core Attribute Learn, it is time to draw some personal conclusions.

STRENGTH:

WHAT HAVE YOU DISCOVERED ABOUT YOURSELF THAT YOU WOULD IDENTIFY AS THE STRONGEST CHARACTERISTIC YOU HAVE REGARDING LEARNING?

Identify areas in your personal or professional life where the strengths that you identified in your Learn core attributes profile could be used as a self-empowering quality that can help further your career or enrich your life.

CHALLENGE:

WHAT COMPONENTS OF LEARNING HAVE YOU IDENTIFIED AS AREAS THAT YOU SHOULD DEVELOP, TO HELP YOU RIGHT NOW? WHAT ACTION WILL YOU CHOOSE TO MAKE THIS HAPPEN?

WHAT ASPECT OF LEARNING HAVE YOU IDENTIFIED AS AN AREA THAT YOU SHOULD IMPROVE UPON TO HELP YOU IN THE FUTURE? WHAT ACTION SHOULD YOU TAKE AND WHEN?

Overall Score

For your *Learn* Assessment Summary, bring forward your individual scores and place them in the appropriate box below. This score will be used later in the chapter, to help you create an action plan for your future.

	I enjoy learning and proactively continue to learn.
	I am interested in people and events.
	I know how to read and find information when I need it.
	I pay attention to societal and work trends that are impacting the future now.
	I know how to filter through essential and non-essential information.

MY TOTAL SCORE:

POSITIVE ATTITUDE AND BEHAVIOR

I have self-esteem and confidence.

DESCRIBE A TIME WHEN YOU WERE WILLING TO EXPRESS YOUR IDEAS, EVEN THOUGH YOU KNEW THAT OTHERS MIGHT DISAGREE.

HOW WOULD YOU DEFINE SELF-ESTEEM?

WHAT METHODS DO YOU USE TO PROACTIVELY DEVELOP YOUR SELF-CONFIDENCE?

WHAT THINGS DO YOU DO BEFORE YOU GO INTO A MEETING TO ENSURE THAT YOU WILL BE SELF-CONFIDENT?

CAN YOU DESCRIBE A TIME WHEN YOU BECAME MORE CONFIDENT AND REALIZED AS A RESULT OF THIS INCREASED CONFIDENCE THAT YOUR SELF-ESTEEM HAD GROWN?

Now rate yourself…be fair, be kind and be honest. Consider your personal life and how it is affected by this attribute. Note *Your Thoughts…*in the space provided at the end of this book.

A. ABILITY
How well is this attribute developed?

1 WEAK	2	3	4	5 STRONG

B. APPLICABILITY
How often do I really demonstrate it?

1 WEAK	2	3	4	5 STRONG

MY SCORE
(A X B)

=

POSITIVE ATTITUDE AND BEHAVIOR

I have a positive attitude toward learning, growth and personal health.

WHAT CONSCIOUS STEPS HAVE YOU TAKEN IN DEVELOPING A POSITIVE ATTITUDE?

HOW DOES THIS BEHAVIOR TOWARDS LEARNING, GROWTH AND PERSONAL HEALTH EXHIBIT ITSELF IN YOUR LIFE?

WHAT DIFFICULTIES HAVE YOU ENCOUNTERED IN MAINTAINING A POSITIVE ATTITUDE?

IF YOU HAVE NOT EXHIBITED POSITIVE BEHAVIOR IN THESE AREAS UNTIL NOW, HOW HAS IT PLAYED OUT IN YOUR LIFE?

Now rate yourself…be fair, be kind and be honest. Consider your personal life and how it is affected by this attribute. Note *Your Thoughts…* in the space provided at the end of this book.

A. ABILITY
How well is this attribute developed?

1 WEAK	2	3	4	5 STRONG

B. APPLICABILITY
How often do I really demonstrate it?

1 WEAK	2	3	4	5 STRONG

MY SCORE
(A X B)

(=)

POSITIVE ATTITUDE AND BEHAVIOR

I am a person of honesty, integrity and personal ethics.

WHAT IS YOUR "TRUTH" REGARDING THE ABOVE STATEMENT?

IDENTIFY A SITUATION WHERE YOUR "SPOKEN" POSITION DID NOT MATCH HOW YOU FELT INTERNALLY AND DESCRIBE HOW THAT MADE YOU FEEL.

WHAT WOULD BE THE PERCEPTION OF OTHERS OF YOUR HONESTY, INTEGRITY AND PERSONAL ETHICS?

HOW DO THE WORDS TRUTH, CANDOR, DISCERNMENT AND DECEPTION RESONATE FOR YOU WHEN DESCRIBING YOURSELF AS A PERSON OF HONESTY, INTEGRITY AND PERSONAL ETHICS?

Now rate yourself...be fair, be kind and be honest. Consider your personal life and how it is affected by this attribute. Note *Your Thoughts...*in the space provided at the end of this book.

A. ABILITY
How well is this attribute developed?

1 WEAK	2	3	4	5 STRONG

B. APPLICABILITY
How often do I really demonstrate it?

1 WEAK	2	3	4	5 STRONG

MY SCORE
(A X B)

=

POSITIVE ATTITUDE AND BEHAVIOR

I have the initiative, energy, tenacity and perseverance to get the job done.

WHAT DOES "GOING THE EXTRA DISTANCE TO GET THE JOB DONE" MEAN TO YOU?

IDENTIFY THREE SITUATIONS WHERE YOUR PERSONAL INITIATIVE PROVIDED THE SPARK AND THE ENERGY TO GET THE JOB DONE.

IN WHAT SITUATIONS ARE YOU SELF-DRIVEN TO GET THE JOB DONE?

DESCRIBE A SITUATION WHERE YOUR TENACITY AND PERSEVERANCE SUSTAINED YOU AND ALLOWED YOU TO GET THE JOB DONE.

IN WHAT SITUATIONS DO YOU RELY ON OR EXPECT OTHERS TO TELL YOU TO GET THE JOB DONE?

Now rate yourself…be fair, be kind and be honest. Consider your personal life and how it is affected by this attribute. Note *Your Thoughts…*in the space provided at the end of this book.

A. ABILITY
How well is this attribute developed?

1	2	3	4	5
WEAK				STRONG

B. APPLICABILITY
How often do I really demonstrate it?

1	2	3	4	5
WEAK				STRONG

MY SCORE
(A X B)

(=)

POSITIVE ATTITUDE AND BEHAVIOR

I use positive self-talk and don't put down people, ideas or opportunities.

HOW DOES YOUR SELF-TALK AFFECT HOW YOU FUNCTION ON THE JOB?

IDENTIFY THREE SCENARIOS WHERE YOUR SELF-TALK HAS CONTRIBUTED POSITIVELY OR NEGATIVELY TO THE OUTCOME OF THE SITUATION.

WHAT METHODS DO YOU USE TO ENSURE THAT YOU DO NOT PUT DOWN PEOPLE, IDEAS OR OPPORTUNITIES?

HOW WOULD OTHER PEOPLE REACT IF YOU STATED, "I DO NOT PUT DOWN PEOPLE, IDEAS OR OPPORTUNITIES?"

Now rate yourself…be fair, be kind and be honest. Consider your personal life and how it is affected by this attribute. Note *Your Thoughts…*in the space provided at the end of this book.

A. ABILITY
How well is this attribute developed?

1	2	3	4	5
WEAK				STRONG

B. APPLICABILITY
How often do I really demonstrate it?

1	2	3	4	5
WEAK				STRONG

MY SCORE
(A X B)

=

Summary Assessment

POSITIVE ATTITUDE AND BEHAVIOR

Now that you have examined the five key components of the Core Attribute Positive Attitude and Behavior, it is time to draw some personal conclusions.

STRENGTH:

WHAT HAVE YOU DISCOVERED ABOUT YOURSELF THAT YOU WOULD IDENTIFY AS THE STRONGEST CHARACTERISTIC YOU HAVE REGARDING POSITIVE ATTITUDE AND BEHAVIOR?

Identify areas in your personal or professional life where the strengths that you identified in your Positive Attitude and Behavior core attributes profile could be used as a self-empowering quality that can help further your career or enrich your life.

CHALLENGE:

WHAT COMPONENTS OF POSITIVE ATTITUDE AND BEHAVIOR HAVE YOU IDENTIFIED AS AREAS THAT YOU SHOULD DEVELOP, TO HELP YOU RIGHT NOW? WHAT ACTION WILL YOU CHOOSE TO MAKE THIS HAPPEN?

WHAT ASPECT OF POSITIVE ATTITUDE AND BEHAVIOR HAVE YOU IDENTIFIED AS AN AREA THAT YOU SHOULD IMPROVE UPON TO HELP YOU IN THE FUTURE? WHAT ACTION SHOULD YOU TAKE AND WHEN?

Overall Score

For your *Positive Attitude and Behavior* Assessment Summary, bring forward your individual scores and place them in the appropriate box below. This score will be used later in the chapter, to help you create an action plan for your future.

	I have self-esteem and confidence.
	I have a positive attitude toward learning, growth and personal health.
	I am a person of honesty, integrity and personal ethics.
	I have the initiative, energy, tenacity and perseverance to get the job done.
	I use positive self-talk and don't put down people, ideas or opportunities.

MY TOTAL SCORE:

RESPONSIBILITY

I set and achieve goals and priorities in work and personal life.

DESCRIBE A TIME WHEN YOU SET GOALS AND PRIORITIES.

DO YOU PUT PRIORITIES IN APPROPRIATE ORDER?

WHAT PROCESS DID YOU USE TO SET THESE GOALS AND PRIORITIES?

HOW DO YOU ENSURE THAT YOU ARE NOT JUST DOING THE EASY THINGS FIRST?

HOW DO YOU ACHIEVE WHAT YOU SET OUT TO DO DAILY, WEEKLY, ANNUALLY?

HOW DO YOU ASSESS WHETHER YOUR GOALS AND PRIORITIES HAVE BEEN ACHIEVED?

Now rate yourself...be fair, be kind and be honest. Consider your personal life and how it is affected by this attribute. Note *Your Thoughts*...in the space provided at the end of this book.

A. ABILITY
How well is this attribute developed?

1	2	3	4	5
WEAK				STRONG

B. APPLICABILITY
How often do I really demonstrate it?

1	2	3	4	5
WEAK				STRONG

MY SCORE
(A X B)

=

RESPONSIBILITY

I accept that I am responsible and accountable in all aspects of my life.

DO YOU AGREE THAT WHEN YOU CHOOSE TO NOT ACCEPT RESPONSIBILITY AND ACCOUNTABILITY FOR YOUR OWN ACTIONS, THAT THE RESPONSIBILITY AND ACCOUNTABILITY FOR THOSE ACTIONS HAS TO BE PLACED SOMEWHERE?

GIVE AN EXAMPLE OF WHEN YOU ACCEPTED PERSONAL RESPONSIBILITY AND ACCOUNTABILITY FOR SOMETHING YOU'D DONE.

FURTHER, DO YOU AGREE THAT MANY TIMES PEOPLE, IN NOT ACCEPTING PERSONAL RESPONSIBILITY AND ACCOUNTABILITY FOR THEIR ACTIONS, CHOOSE TO BLAME OR SHAME ANOTHER?

IN WHAT CIRCUMSTANCES DO YOU FIND YOURSELF HOLDING SOMEONE ELSE ACCOUNTABLE BECAUSE YOU THINK THEY SHOULD BE ABLE TO READ YOUR MIND AND KNOW WHAT YOU'RE FEELING?

HOW WOULD YOU RECOGNIZE IF YOU HAVE A PATTERN OF OFF-LOADING YOUR "INTELLECTUAL AND EMOTIONAL BAGGAGE" ONTO OTHERS?

Now rate yourself...be fair, be kind and be honest. Consider your personal life and how it is affected by this attribute. Note *Your Thoughts...* in the space provided at the end of this book.

A. ABILITY
How well is this attribute developed?

1 WEAK	2	3	4	5 STRONG

B. APPLICABILITY
How often do I really demonstrate it?

1 WEAK	2	3	4	5 STRONG

MY SCORE
(A X B)

=

RESPONSIBILITY

I can plan and manage my time.

HOW DO YOU KNOW YOU MANAGE YOUR TIME WELL?

HOW DO YOU USE A DAYTIMER OR PLANNER TO PLAN YOUR TIME EFFECTIVELY?

WHEN YOU DON'T MANAGE YOUR TIME WELL, HOW DO YOU PUT YOUR PLANS BACK ON TRACK?

HOW DO YOU BALANCE WORK TIME, LEISURE TIME AND PERSONAL TIME?

Now rate yourself…be fair, be kind and be honest. Consider your personal life and how it is affected by this attribute. Note *Your Thoughts*…in the space provided at the end of this book.

A. ABILITY
How well is this attribute developed?

| 1 WEAK | 2 | 3 | 4 | 5 STRONG |

B. APPLICABILITY
How often do I really demonstrate it?

| 1 WEAK | 2 | 3 | 4 | 5 STRONG |

MY SCORE
(A X B)

(=)

RESPONSIBILITY

I can handle my financial resources for today and know that I must plan for my own financial future.

WHAT PERSONAL BUDGETING TECHNIQUES HAVE WORKED FOR YOU?

HOW HAVE YOU MANAGED YOUR FINANCIAL PLANS TO TAKE YOU THROUGH THIS MONTH, THE NEXT SIX MONTHS AND YOUR RETIREMENT?

WHAT ASPECTS OF THESE TECHNIQUES HAVE FAILED AND WHY?

WHAT CONTINGENCY PLANS DO YOU HAVE FOR FUTURE MAJOR EXPENSES OR REDUCTION OF INCOME?

Now rate yourself...be fair, be kind and be honest. Consider your personal life and how it is affected by this attribute. Note *Your Thoughts...* in the space provided at the end of this book.

A. ABILITY
How well is this attribute developed?

| 1 WEAK | 2 | 3 | 4 | 5 STRONG |

B. APPLICABILITY
How often do I really demonstrate it?

| 1 WEAK | 2 | 3 | 4 | 5 STRONG |

MY SCORE
(A X B)

(=)

RESPONSIBILITY

I accept that I am in control of my own career choices and should not relinquish that responsibility.

DESCRIBE AN OCCASION WHEN YOU CONSCIOUSLY OR UNCONSCIOUSLY RELINQUISHED RESPONSIBILITY FOR YOUR CAREER.

HOW HAS THIS SENSE OF PERSONAL CONTROL BEEN REFLECTED IN YOUR CAREER CHOICES TO DATE?

DO YOU FIND THAT MANY PEOPLE YOU WORK WITH ARE RESENTFUL THAT 'JOBS FOR LIFE' ARE RAPIDLY BECOMING A THING OF THE PAST? WHAT IS YOUR RESPONSE TO THEIR ANGER?

WHAT STEPS HAVE YOU TAKEN TO AVOID THE "I'M STUCK, I HAVE NO CHOICES" TRAP?

Now rate yourself…be fair, be kind and be honest. Consider your personal life and how it is affected by this attribute. Note *Your Thoughts*…in the space provided at the end of this book.

A. ABILITY
How well is this attribute developed?

1 WEAK	2	3	4	5 STRONG

B. APPLICABILITY
How often do I really demonstrate it?

1 WEAK	2	3	4	5 STRONG

MY SCORE
(A X B)

(=)

Summary Assessment

RESPONSIBILITY

Now that you have examined the five key components of the Core Attribute Responsibility, it is time to draw some personal conclusions.

STRENGTH:

WHAT HAVE YOU DISCOVERED ABOUT YOURSELF THAT YOU WOULD IDENTIFY AS THE STRONGEST CHARACTERISTIC YOU HAVE REGARDING RESPONSIBILITY?

Identify areas in your personal or professional life where the strengths that you identified in your Responsibility core attributes profile could be used as a self-empowering quality that can help further your career or enrich your life.

CHALLENGE:

WHAT COMPONENTS OF RESPONSIBILITY HAVE YOU IDENTIFIED AS AREAS THAT YOU SHOULD DEVELOP, TO HELP YOU RIGHT NOW? WHAT ACTION WILL YOU CHOOSE TO MAKE THIS HAPPEN?

WHAT ASPECT OF RESPONSIBILITY HAVE YOU IDENTIFIED AS AN AREA THAT YOU SHOULD IMPROVE UPON TO HELP YOU IN THE FUTURE? WHAT ACTION SHOULD YOU TAKE AND WHEN?

Overall Score

For your *Responsibility* Assessment Summary, bring forward your individual scores and place them in the appropriate box below. This score will be used later in the chapter, to help you create an action plan for your future.

	I set and achieve goals and priorities in work and personal life.
	I accept that I am responsible and accountable in all aspects of my life.
	I can plan and manage my time.
	I can handle my financial resources for today and know I must plan for my own financial future.
	I accept that I am in control of my career choices and should not relinquish responsibility.

MY TOTAL SCORE:

ADAPTABILITY

I have a willingness to accept change and describe myself as flexible and adaptable.

DO YOU DESCRIBE YOURSELF AS A "GO WITH THE FLOW" PERSON? WHY?

IDENTIFY A RECENT SITUATION INVOLVING CHANGE THAT YOU DIDN'T INITIATE OR CONTROL AND HOW YOU FELT ABOUT IT.

DO YOU HAVE THE ABILITY TO SEE OPPORTUNITIES WITHIN CHANGE?

WERE YOUR FEELINGS VALID OR WERE YOU JUST BEING RESISTANT AS A MATTER OF COURSE?

DESCRIBE A TIME WHEN YOU DEMONSTRATED A WILLINGNESS TO CHANGE.

HOW WOULD OTHERS VIEW YOUR FLEXIBILITY AND ADAPTABILITY?

Now rate yourself…be fair, be kind and be honest. Consider your personal life and how it is affected by this attribute. Note *Your Thoughts*…in the space provided at the end of this book.

A. ABILITY
How well is this attribute developed?

| 1 WEAK | 2 | 3 | 4 | 5 STRONG |

B. APPLICABILITY
How often do I really demonstrate it?

| 1 WEAK | 2 | 3 | 4 | 5 STRONG |

MY SCORE
(A X B)

=

ADAPTABILITY

I recognize and respect people's diversity and individual differences.

WHAT IN YOUR OPINION ARE THE KEY SOCIETAL ISSUES THAT YOU WOULD ASSOCIATE WITH PEOPLE'S DIVERSITY AND INDIVIDUAL DIFFERENCES?

IN YOUR OPINION WHAT ARE THE KEY DIFFERENCES BETWEEN MALE AND FEMALE MANAGERS AND/OR COWORKERS THAT ARE A CAUSE OF OFFICE PROBLEMS?

WHEN WOULD YOU KNOW THAT PEOPLE'S DIVERSITY AND INDIVIDUAL DIFFERENCES ARE RESPECTED?

HOW IS YOUR ANSWER INFLUENCED BY PERSONALITY TRAITS AND/OR STEREOTYPICAL ATTRIBUTES? WHY?

IN DEFINING YOURSELF AS A TRADITIONAL OR PROGRESSIVE THINKER, COMPLETE THIS SENTENCE: "I WOULD EMPHASIZE THAT..."

WHEN SOMEONE DISAGREES WITH YOUR OPINION HOW DO YOU REACT (IN YOUR MIND)? BE SPECIFIC.

WHAT DO YOU DO WHEN YOU REALIZE PEOPLE'S DIVERSITY AND INDIVIDUAL DIFFERENCES ARE NOT BEING RESPECTED?

Now rate yourself...be fair, be kind and be honest. Consider your personal life and how it is affected by this attribute. Note *Your Thoughts...* in the space provided at the end of this book.

A. ABILITY
How well is this attribute developed?

| 1 WEAK | 2 | 3 | 4 | 5 STRONG |

B. APPLICABILITY
How often do I really demonstrate it?

| 1 WEAK | 2 | 3 | 4 | 5 STRONG |

MY SCORE
(A X B)

(=)

ADAPTABILITY

I can identify and suggest new ideas.

HAVE I TRAINED MY MIND TO SEE OPPORTUNITIES? WHEN HAVE I USED THIS SKILL?

DO YOU WILLINGLY PARTICIPATE IN SHARING NEW IDEAS?

ARE YOU ABLE TO OFFER BUILDING BLOCKS OF IDEAS OR CONCEPTS TO ENHANCE OTHERS' IDEAS?

ARE YOU WILLING TO DO THAT?

Now rate yourself…be fair, be kind and be honest. Consider your personal life and how it is affected by this attribute. Note *Your Thoughts…*in the space provided at the end of this book.

A. ABILITY
How well is this attribute developed?

1	2	3	4	5
WEAK				STRONG

B. APPLICABILITY
How often do I really demonstrate it?

1	2	3	4	5
WEAK				STRONG

MY SCORE
(A X B)

=

ADAPTABILITY

I am a creative contributor.

HOW DO YOU TRY TO THINK BEYOND TRADITIONAL SOLUTIONS?

WHAT DO YOU DO TO NURTURE YOUR CREATIVITY?

DO YOU TAKE THE TIME TO LOOK EXTERNALLY FOR NEW IDEAS?

DESCRIBE A TIME WHEN YOU HAD A CREATIVE IDEA ACCEPTED.

WHAT METHODS HAVE YOU DEVELOPED TO SIFT THROUGH AND SAVE GOOD "POTENTIAL" IDEAS?

HOW DO YOU REACT WHEN YOUR CREATIVE IDEAS ARE REJECTED?

HOW DO YOU RESEARCH CREATIVE IDEAS BEFORE PRESENTING THEM?

HOW DO YOU RESPOND IN SUCH A SITUATION?

Now rate yourself...be fair, be kind and be honest. Consider your personal life and how it is affected by this attribute. Note *Your Thoughts*...in the space provided at the end of this book.

A. ABILITY
How well is this attribute developed?

| 1 WEAK | 2 | 3 | 4 | 5 STRONG |

B. APPLICABILITY
How often do I really demonstrate it?

| 1 WEAK | 2 | 3 | 4 | 5 STRONG |

MY SCORE
(A X B)

(=)

ADAPTABILITY

I see my mistakes as learning experiences.

IN THE FACE OF MISTAKES DO YOU CONTINUE TO TRY OR DO YOU SHUT DOWN?

HOW HAS VIEWING MISTAKES AS A PERSONAL FAILURE PLAYED OUT IN YOUR LIFE?

DO YOU PUT YOURSELF DOWN FOR MAKING MISTAKES?

DO YOU SIMPLY TRY TO "WING IT" TOO MANY TIMES?

WHEN YOU HAVE MADE A MISTAKE, WAS IT A FUNCTION OF NOT BEING FULLY PREPARED OR NOT KNOWING WHAT YOU WERE DOING? WHAT HAPPENED?

WHAT HAS BEEN THE COST OF JUST "WINGING IT"?

WHEN HAVE YOU TAKEN THE TIME IN THE LAST SIX MONTHS TO TRULY ASSESS AND IDENTIFY AREAS FOR IMPROVEMENT?

Now rate yourself...be fair, be kind and be honest. Consider your personal life and how it is affected by this attribute. Note *Your Thoughts*...in the space provided at the end of this book.

A. ABILITY
How well is this attribute developed?

| 1 WEAK | 2 | 3 | 4 | 5 STRONG |

B. APPLICABILITY
How often do I really demonstrate it?

| 1 WEAK | 2 | 3 | 4 | 5 STRONG |

MY SCORE
(A X B)

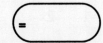

=

Summary Assessment

ADAPTABILITY

Now that you have examined the five key components of the Core Attribute Adaptability, it is time to draw some personal conclusions.

STRENGTH:

WHAT HAVE YOU DISCOVERED ABOUT YOURSELF THAT YOU WOULD IDENTIFY AS THE STRONGEST CHARACTERISTIC YOU HAVE REGARDING ADAPTABILITY?

Identify areas in your personal or professional life where the strengths that you identified in your Adaptability core attributes profile could be used as a self-empowering quality that can help further your career or enrich your life.

CHALLENGE:

WHAT COMPONENTS OF ADAPTABILITY HAVE YOU IDENTIFIED AS AREAS THAT YOU SHOULD DEVELOP, TO HELP YOU RIGHT NOW? WHAT ACTION WILL YOU CHOOSE TO MAKE THIS HAPPEN?

WHAT ASPECT OF ADAPTABILITY HAVE YOU IDENTIFIED AS AN AREA THAT YOU SHOULD IMPROVE UPON TO HELP YOU IN THE FUTURE? WHAT ACTION SHOULD YOU TAKE AND WHEN?

Overall Score

For your *Adaptability* Assessment Summary, bring forward your individual scores and place them in the appropriate box below. This score will be used later in the chapter, to help you create an action plan for your future.

	I have a willingness to accept change and describe myself as flexible and adaptable.
	I recognize and respect people's diversity and individual differences.
	I can identify and suggest new ideas.
	I am a creative contributor.
	I see my mistakes as learning experiences.

MY TOTAL SCORE:

TEAMWORK

I can work within the culture of a group or organization

ARE THERE POLICIES AND/OR PEOPLE THAT SIMPLY IRRITATE YOU?

DESCRIBE A SITUATION THAT ENABLED YOU TO SEE GOOD TEAMWORK IN ACTION.

WHAT DOES THE EXPRESSION "UNWRITTEN RULES OF THE ORGANIZATION" MEAN TO YOU?

DESCRIBE A TIME WHEN YOU WERE EFFECTIVELY ABLE TO FUNCTION IN A TEAM SETTING.

DESCRIBE A SITUATION WHEN YOU WERE IMPACTED POSITIVELY OR NEGATIVELY BY THESE UNWRITTEN RULES.

WHAT ARE YOUR GREATEST CONTRIBUTING ASSETS TO A TEAM SITUATION?

IN WHAT AREAS DO YOU NEED TO IMPROVE TO FUNCTION MORE FULLY IN A TEAM ENVIRONMENT?

WHAT HAS YOUR SCHOOL AND WORK EXPERIENCE TAUGHT YOU ABOUT TEAMWORK?

Now rate yourself…be fair, be kind and be honest. Consider your personal life and how it is affected by this attribute. Note *Your Thoughts…*in the space provided at the end of this book.

A. ABILITY
How well is this attribute developed?

| 1 WEAK | 2 | 3 | 4 | 5 STRONG |

B. APPLICABILITY
How often do I really demonstrate it?

| 1 WEAK | 2 | 3 | 4 | 5 STRONG |

MY SCORE
(A X B)

=

TEAMWORK

I respect the thoughts and opinions of others.

IN A TEAM SETTING HOW WOULD YOU DESCRIBE YOUR REACTION TO OPINIONS THAT DIFFER FROM YOURS?

HOW OFTEN DO YOU INITIATE DRAWING OUT THE OPINIONS OF LESS VOCAL TEAM MEMBERS?

ARE YOU OPEN TO NEW IDEAS, WAYS OR PROCEDURES?

HOW DO YOU LET OTHER TEAM MEMBERS KNOW THEIR THOUGHTS AND OPINIONS ARE A VALUABLE CONTRIBUTION?

HOW WOULD YOU DRAW OUT THE OPINIONS OF LESS VOCAL TEAM MEMBERS?

WHEN LISTENING TO OTHERS...ARE YOU SINCERELY INTERESTED IN WHAT THEY ARE SAYING OR ARE YOU BUSY THINKING ABOUT WHAT YOU'RE GOING TO SAY?

WHAT SKILLS HAVE YOU DEVELOPED THAT HELP ENSURE THAT THE THOUGHTS AND OPINIONS OF OTHERS ARE BEING RESPECTED?

DO YOU GIVE OTHERS THE OPPORTUNITY TO COMPLETELY EXPRESS THEIR VIEWS OR DO YOU TRY TO INTERRUPT TO GET YOUR THOUGHTS IN THE CONVERSATION?

Now rate yourself...be fair, be kind and be honest. Consider your personal life and how it is affected by this attribute. Note *Your Thoughts...* in the space provided at the end of this book.

A. ABILITY
How well is this attribute developed?

| 1 WEAK | 2 | 3 | 4 | 5 STRONG |

B. APPLICABILITY
How often do I really demonstrate it?

| 1 WEAK | 2 | 3 | 4 | 5 STRONG |

MY SCORE
(A X B)

(=)

TEAMWORK

I can accept a team decision or direction and support it, even when I don't agree.

DO YOU CHALLENGE OTHERS BY SPEAKING AGAINST THEM? DO YOU CHALLENGE THEIR IDEAS BEHIND THEIR BACKS OR TO THEIR FACE?

WHAT SKILLS ARE YOU CURRENTLY DEVELOPING THAT WILL ASSIST YOU IN BEING A BETTER TEAM MEMBER?

DESCRIBE A TIME WHEN YOU GOT BEHIND A TEAM DECISION EVEN IF YOU DID NOT TOTALLY AGREE.

WERE YOU ABLE TO LIVE WITH THIS GRACEFULLY OR DID YOU RESPOND IN AN INAPPROPRIATE MANNER?

IF YOU ARE NOT PLEASED WITH HOW YOU ARE HANDLING TEAM DECISIONS, WHAT ARE YOU DOING ABOUT IT?

IF YOU FIND YOU ARE CONSTANTLY OPPOSING OR CONTRADICTING TEAM DECISIONS, HAVE YOU EVER CONSIDERED THAT YOU MIGHT BE THE PROBLEM? IF SO...WHAT NOW?

Now rate yourself...be fair, be kind and be honest. Consider your personal life and how it is affected by this attribute. Note *Your Thoughts...* in the space provided at the end of this book.

A. ABILITY
How well is this attribute developed?

| 1 WEAK | 2 | 3 | 4 | 5 STRONG |

B. APPLICABILITY
How often do I really demonstrate it?

| 1 WEAK | 2 | 3 | 4 | 5 STRONG |

MY SCORE
(A X B)

=

TEAMWORK

I can exercise "give and take" and seek a team approach.

DO YOU EVER JUST LET OTHERS HAVE THEIR OWN WAY BECAUSE IT'S TOO MUCH EFFORT TO FIGHT FOR WHAT YOU WANT OR TOO DIFFICULT TO CHALLENGE THEM?

DO YOU HAVE MORE DIFFICULTY WITH "GIVE AND TAKE" BEHAVIOR IN YOUR PERSONAL OR YOUR WORK LIFE?

DESCRIBE A TIME WHEN YOU FELT IT WAS GOOD JUDGMENT TO LET OTHERS GET THEIR OWN WAY.

IN WHAT SITUATIONS HAVE YOU SEEN "GIVE AND TAKE" BEHAVIOR MODELED IN A POSITIVE MANNER?

HOW DO YOU FEEL WHEN YOU LET OTHERS GET THEIR OWN WAY FOR NO VALID REASON?

Now rate yourself…be fair, be kind and be honest. Consider your personal life and how it is affected by this attribute. Note *Your Thoughts...* in the space provided at the end of this book.

A. ABILITY
How well is this attribute developed?

1 WEAK　2　3　4　5 STRONG

B. APPLICABILITY
How often do I really demonstrate it?

1 WEAK　2　3　4　5 STRONG

MY SCORE
(A X B)

=

TEAMWORK

I can lead when appropriate.

IN WHAT SITUATIONS DO YOU TEND TO TAKE CHARGE WHERE OTHER PEOPLE ARE INVOLVED?

HOW WOULD YOU GIVE OTHERS THE OPPORTUNITY TO LEAD WHEN THEY ARE THE MOST SUITED?

WHAT WOULD BE YOUR BASIC MOTIVATION IN ASSUMING THAT YOU SHOULD TAKE CHARGE IN THESE SITUATIONS?

HOW DO YOU KNOW WHEN TO GIVE OTHERS THE OPPORTUNITY TO LEAD, WHEN IT WOULD BE A GROWTH OPPORTUNITY FOR THEM AND YOURSELF?

IN YOUR PAST, HAS THAT MINDSET CAUSED TROUBLE FOR YOU IN YOUR RELATIONSHIPS WITH OTHERS?

DO YOU ALWAYS KNOW YOU ARE RIGHT? (AND ARE YOU?)

Now rate yourself…be fair, be kind and be honest. Consider your personal life and how it is affected by this attribute. Note *Your Thoughts…*in the space provided at the end of this book.

A. ABILITY
How well is this attribute developed?

1 WEAK	2	3	4	5 STRONG

B. APPLICABILITY
How often do I really demonstrate it?

1 WEAK	2	3	4	5 STRONG

MY SCORE
(A X B)

(=)

Summary Assessment

TEAMWORK

Now that you have examined the five key components of the Core Attribute Teamwork, it is time to draw some personal conclusions.

STRENGTH:

WHAT HAVE YOU DISCOVERED ABOUT YOURSELF THAT YOU WOULD IDENTIFY AS THE STRONGEST CHARACTERISTIC YOU HAVE REGARDING TEAMWORK?

Identify areas in your personal or professional life where the strengths that you identified in your Teamwork core attributes profile could be used as a self-empowering quality that can help further your career or enrich your life.

CHALLENGE:

WHAT COMPONENTS OF TEAMWORK HAVE YOU IDENTIFIED AS AREAS THAT YOU SHOULD DEVELOP, TO HELP YOU RIGHT NOW? WHAT ACTION WILL YOU CHOOSE TO MAKE THIS HAPPEN?

WHAT ASPECT OF TEAMWORK HAVE YOU IDENTIFIED AS AN AREA THAT YOU SHOULD IMPROVE UPON TO HELP YOU IN THE FUTURE? WHAT ACTION SHOULD YOU TAKE AND WHEN?

Overall Score

For your *Teamwork* Assessment Summary, bring forward your individual scores and place them in the appropriate box below. This score will be used later in the chapter, to help you create an action plan for your future.

	I can work within the culture of a group or organization.
	I respect the thoughts and opinions of others.
	I can accept a team decision or direction and support it, even when I don't agree.
	I can exercise 'give and take' and seek a team approach.
	I can lead when appropriate.

MY TOTAL SCORE:

Core attributes self-assessment summary

You have now completed your Core Attributes self-assessment and should have a good sense of your strengths and challenges in these core areas. As you continue to work through this workbook, you will use this information to help create a personal strategy as part of your overall career and personal life management plan. As you develop your plan, keep in mind that these are the behaviors and aptitudes that employers want to see in their employees.

Personal development action plan

In completing your self-evaluation you were given the opportunity to make definitive observations about your natural strengths and what you identified as personal challenges where you should improve.

You can make observations about yourself and intellectually say, "I really should do something about that" or "I'll get around to it." However, just thinking about what you should do and not taking any tangible action leaves everything as 'just thoughts'. Writing down tangible ideas or goals is important! They become constant reminders of what you want to change or improve.

This is not an exercise to finish just for the sake of finishing. The results of this exercise are the foundation of your personal development action plan. It is meant to be a dynamic document. We advise that you use it as a periodic reminder and a re-assessment tool of what you have actually done to advance your plan.

Bring forward your scores

At the conclusion of each section you totaled your scores for each specific Core Attribute. Bring forward your total scores from each of the Core Attribute assessments and place your score next to each skill.

_____Communicate

_____Think

_____Learn

_____Positive Attitude and Behavior

_____Responsibility

_____Adaptability

_____Teamwork

As you proceed with the development of this action plan, you will want to frequently refer to the specifics you identified as your strengths and challenges for each Core Attribute.

First look

WHAT DO YOU SEE WHEN YOU TAKE A LOOK AT ALL THE CORE ATTRIBUTES AT ONE TIME? DO YOU SEE A SPECIFIC ASPECT OR PATTERN EMERGING THAT HAS INFLUENCED YOUR WORK LIFE? WHAT ABOUT YOUR PERSONAL LIFE?

DO YOU SEE HOW YOUR PROFICIENCY RELATIVE TO THE DIFFERENT CORE ATTRIBUTES MAY HAVE WORKED TOGETHER (POSITIVELY OR NEGATIVELY) IN INFLUENCING YOUR CAREER CHOICES AND OPTIONS?

Plan your plan...work your plan

Everyone approaches personal development and goal setting differently. Some people like very detailed lists and goals. Others prefer to take a broader overall assessment approach. Still others don't want to deal with long lists because they find them intimidating or discouraging. The following options take these preferences into consideration.

Option 1 (The "first things first" approach)

This approach will help you achieve a new goal quickly. You can then use the energy generated by accomplishing this fast-found achievement to power your resolve to handle the harder personal development goals. The point is you want to have a strategic approach for putting your plan into action.

For this option, assume that your strongest attribute is serving you well! Identify your "first things first" goal from your second strongest attribute.

I have always had a great gift for being adaptable. Put me in any situation and I seem to be able to successfully float to the surface. I have never used this skill to consciously build and develop the skills of my subordinates.

Adaptability:	*"I respect people's individuality and diversity."*
My goal is:	*to show Helen that I value her cultural contribution to our weekly meetings.*
My approach:	*at Tuesday's meeting I will find an opportunity to do this*
Will achieve this:	*by the end of this week*

2nd STRONGEST ATTRIBUTE: _____
- My goal is:
- My approach to achieve this:
- I will achieve this by: (at most two to four weeks)

Once you have completed this process for your second highest scoring attribute, use the new-found energy and resolve you gained from realizing this goal and follow the same process for your two weaker Attributes. You can set these as intermediate and long-term goals.

2nd LOWEST SCORE ATTRIBUTE: _____
  • My goal is:
  • My approach to achieve this:
  • I will achieve this by: (maximum two to three months)

LOWEST SCORE ATTRIBUTE: _____
  • My goal is:
  • My approach to achieve this:
  • I will achieve this by: (maximum three to six months)

Option 2 (Build on your strengths approach)

Challenge yourself to find creative solutions from within. Pick your own brain! Look at the seven attributes. Using your intuitive and creative abilities, tap into your greatest strengths (e.g. highest scoring attributes Learn and Communicate) to help you find solutions to your greatest challenges (e.g. lowest scoring attributes Responsibility and Adaptability). Find your answers from within. Record the two highest scoring attributes on the left and the two lowest scoring attributes on the right. Review the exercises you completed as part of the Core Attributes Self assessment process and identify three key words or phrases that will clearly 'frame' your strengths and your challenges.

Example:
My great strengths are my ability to Learn and my ability to Communicate. Unfortunately, I find myself to be easily thrown in situations where I am asked to be creative (Adaptability) and to take charge (Responsibility) for delivering unplanned information within a specified time frame.

Since I am so good at learning things quickly, once I identify what I want to learn, I am going to research out a program on creative idea development (Adaptability). At the next opportunity, once I have completed the program, I will proactively present information under circumstances I have normally avoided (Responsibility).

MY HIGHEST SCORE ATTRIBUTES   **MY LOWEST SCORE ATTRIBUTES**

LEARN   **ADAPTABILITY**
1. Enjoy learning   1. Bridge to new ideas
2. Enjoy learning new software   2. Often resist changes
3. Keep up with world news   3. Don't speak during brainstorming

COMMUNICATE   **RESPONSIBILITY**
1. I can make technical presentations   1. I don't set/achieve goals well
2. I can prepare reports   2. I tend to hold others responsible
3. I can interpret instructions well   3. Time management can sometimes be a concern

Now It's Your Turn

YOUR HIGHEST SCORE ATTRIBUTES   **YOUR LOWEST SCORE ATTRIBUTES**

_____   _____

1)   1)

2)   2)

3)   3)

_____   _____

1)   1)

2)   2)

3)   3)

Take a close look and ask yourself how you can use your strengths to augment your efforts in facing your challenges. WHAT ARE THE SOURCES OF STRENGTH AND WISDOM THAT YOU CAN IDENTIFY FROM THE LEFT SIDE TO AUGMENT YOUR RESOLVE TO ADDRESS YOUR CHALLENGES ON THE RIGHT SIDE?

Option 3 (Make it Work for You NOW)

Pick just one attribute that is important to you. Ask yourself what action you need to take to make a difference right away. Set out a highly detailed personal development action plan relative to that one attribute. Take strong, swift action.

I have always been very afraid of public speaking. I also have a strong sense that if I don't do something about this I am going to miss out on a great promotion. In our company all the successful people I know are good public speakers. I am going to join the company public speaking program for six months. I will ask them to help me set achievable goals. I will do this today.

CORE ATTRIBUTE: _____

My goal is: _____

My tasks are: _____

My benchmarks for success are (i.e. I will know I have accomplished this goal when)

_____

My time frame is: _____

Managing My Development is a powerful process. If you have been able to complete the exercises as outlined to your satisfaction, you now have a solid framework for making ongoing decisions regarding your personal growth and empowerment.

 ~ Know that you are not alone ~

There is great support available to you as you pursue meaningful work...the Entrepreneurial Way. There are many like you in the workplace who are more than ready to address some of the issues presented in this book. Perhaps you have friends who would be interested in being more fulfilled and more balanced in their career and personal lives. Why not connect with a group of like-minded people? Each of you will be able to support the other and learn constructive ways of moving each other forward. The energy of the individual can be greatly augmented by the synergy of the group.

🏃 Your plans...

HOPE IS THE PROMISE OF THE FUTURE

Hope is the promise of the future.

 ~ It is so much easier for all of us to find meaning in our work when the environment and culture we work in supports the human person. This story offers hope in what could be...a vision of the future, if you will. If everyone regardless of rank or title chose to do their part to make the workplace a kinder place, meaningful, productive work would be a by-product...because people would enjoy coming to work, and that in itself would be meaningful ~

⚓ What Was Lost Can Be Found ⚓

Long, long ago, soon after the demise of Greece and shortly before the Fall of Rome, a little known culture flourished and was known as the Kingdom of Galzon. As our story begins, we join a group of concerned citizens of Galzon as they gather round the fire in the early hours of the morning - tense, confused and lacking a clear sense of what to do next.

Something was wrong! It was as if everyone in Galzon had fallen under a spell - a spell that affected every aspect of life in the Kingdom. Our tiny band of concerned citizens began by pondering on memories of better days.

It had started first in the fields, where people toiled day in and day out. King Ocko, in his time, did not like how work was being done and he believed that it was important to find another way. He believed that when people worked in the fields - that what they did was important. Thus he made every effort to make sure that those at the top of THEIR field would give their workers the right tools to work with, correct instructions, proper encouragement for work well done and an open mind to any suggestions on how the job could be done better.

The result of this brand of worker-care was a Kingdom that was so productive that every year exceeded the expectations of the year before. Each year King Ocko decreed that, with his blessing and support, all Galzons who helped create this richness for the Kingdom would be encouraged to learn new skills, so they would never grow bored in their work. Further, he decreed that they take time to renew themselves. In this way the workers could continue their good work and do that work in a meaningful way.

Now those who did the King's work and followed his good guidance responded to this treatment in most interesting ways. Often the OcKo-workers, as they were called, could be seen smiling and singing as they approached their field for their day's work. People spoke to one another…and actually seemed to listen and care. These workers felt pride, thought their work meaningful and fun!

This way of working seemed to create its own energy. On work breaks, which King Ocko insisted upon, some workers decided to plant flowers around the edges of one of the fields. Those seeds sown with pride and personal effort given freely, created a 'circle of satisfaction' around that field. The practice of planting flowers took seed, and ultimately, beautiful blossoms that served to beautify and nurture the workplace surrounded every field in the Kingdom. So for the workers, their leaders and for King Ocko who was deeply loved…all was truly well in the world.

Our friends around the early morning fire reminisced and sadly recalled the day King Ocko was slain. For it will always be thus that the light of fairness and respect will shine forth until powerful others say "no more", and thus it was that the Kingdom of Galzon fell to the hands of those who valued profit over people and power over a shared vision.

All manner of things changed in the fields. It was subtle at first; you hardly noticed until too late that the smiling and the singing was no more. There did not seem to be very much to sing about, less to speak about and finally all listening stopped. For who listens when no one cares to hear the tale of woe about improper tools, longer work hours, reduced time for renewal and no interest in creative suggestions…just work, work and more work.

And the fields, something had happened to the fields. Once again it happened slowly, so slowly…it was subtle but it nonetheless happened. The fields, which had always nurtured the kingdom, were no longer respected and valued - worker and workplace no longer producing to capacity…one would not and the other could not. One day the 'circle of satisfaction' bloomed brightly and the next…it was as if it went to seed and was transformed into a 'prison of pain'.

Dear ones, please understand…all is not lost. The hope for the Kingdom of Galzon rests in the hands and hearts of our band of early morning visionaries, the concerned in the Kingdom who know something is deeply wrong. These citizens have a deep desire to return to the wisdom days of King Ocko and carry within them his deeply held belief that wellness in their workplace will be theirs if they can be fully aware of their current reality, vision where they wish to be and choose to take the steps to make it happen.

What Was Lost Can Be Found if we remember that wellness is an organic process. To birth wellness into 'being' it takes leadership, it takes intention and it takes time and above all it takes people very much like yourselves to make it happen.

POST SCRIPT

⚐ *A story worth the telling* ⚐

I was in the process of making the final arrangements to self-publish this book. My year had been complicated and the decision to self-publish had been many months in the making. Then the unimaginable happened. After a very disturbing personal telephone conversation, I took a bit of time to recoup and assure myself that what had transpired in the conversation wasn't going to bother me. Within an hour my right arm was completely immobilized. I was to learn later that I had had an emotional trauma that resulted in a pinched nerve and a frozen shoulder. I suppose one first goes into shock and then for me, fear took over. What if this was it for the rest of my life? One can imagine all the ghastly scenarios that play out from there. With great difficulty, I called myself back to the present moment and step by step, over the next months, I found the help that I needed.

From the outset I had an amazing sense that I would be fine...but the reality of not being able to use my dominant right arm was truly daunting.

Two days later I got a call from the distributor who said that if I was going ahead with self-publishing my book, they would need my book cover design in a week. He also said the book would have to be at the printer by mid-February. In that moment I had to make a choice. Would I take the risk? Did I have the commitment to the project? Somewhere deep inside me I knew what I needed to do and as wild as it now seems I said, "Yes, the cover will be ready next week."

I realized immediately that I had just agreed to revise a book with my writing arm immobilized. Why I thought I could do this I do not know. All I knew was that it was time for this book to be out in the world. The message was important. My being physically challenged didn't seem to be a reason not to get the book ready. For weeks I worked using my non-dominant left hand for my longhand notes and I changed my mouse to the left-hand side for data input. I was amazed how the legibility of my handwriting improved. One-handed typing is a challenge, period.

Everything I did took so much more time. I had to pay attention to things I hadn't paid attention to for years. Getting socks on was a monumental struggle, making meals a time-consuming challenge and washing my hair, always a point of personal pride, became completely overwhelming. To put it in perspective, think of having your dominant arm strapped tight to your side...it is hard to imagine how it affects your life, until you live it.

I was humbled by the experience, particularly when I came to realize how few steps there are between dependence and independence. I will never see life in exactly the same way again. Whomever I believed myself to be before this experience, the person who will emerge on the other side will be a different Judee.

Day by day as I moved closer and closer to my old self, I realized how easy it is to become immobilized by life...to squander precious energy lamenting the cards dealt to us. With energy stores thus depleted, we lack what is needed to engage in a life fully lived.

*Stepping into this life-changing event allowed me to experience how immensely creative one can be in a time of crisis and to understand that even when immobilized, some part of you works. The lesson seems to be, find what works and move. Don't get stuck and don't settle, for it is in the moving that we advance our vision and create the hope we need to sustain ourselves...
especially in the tough times.*

⚡ Your thoughts...

Post note:

As I read this story, I realize that being presented with this experience, I was given the opportunity to live what this book is about. Making the choice to write the book, in my pursuit of meaningful work, at a time that ostensibly was the worst time ever, vastly contributed in fact to my healing process. I can assure you after what I had been through in the last six years, I could have easily shut down and gone to that place that says "this is not fair." I guess the point was, fair or not fair, it was what it was. Accepting what was on my plate made the whole encounter far easier than railing about why it had happened in the first place.

By choosing to write the book, I had purpose and passion and a vision of the future. I was then able to use my energy in constructive, creative ways…and miraculously my energy kept coming. The experience had all the drama of the roller coaster ride through the unknown of a difficult transition. I did not know I would be OK but I had an unshakable sense of hope that I would be. I had a mentor who inspired and guided me, encouraging me to take one step at a time. Most of the time I kept moving, and when I felt myself sliding into dark places…I consciously brought myself back to stay in the present moment. That was and is the only moment I or anyone knows for certain.

In the end, I realized that I had followed my own advice as laid out in this book. As I look back I see that I took the necessary steps to integrate my career and personal life management, so that I might produce a book and find my way to wholeness and well-being. For me, the process was an effort of great magnitude. But the entrepreneurial path I followed was not unknown to me for I have followed it many times throughout my life. I know it works and once again it served me well.

So I will end as I began, saying that a life fully lived takes effort. Every time you make that effort you are further prepared for the next time and for that I am grateful and believe me…you will be too.

Bibliography and Recommended Reading

Bolles, Richard Nelson. *What Color is Your Parachute?* Berkeley, California: Ten Speed Press, 1996.

Bridges, William. Managing Transitions. Reading, Massachusetts: Addison-Wesley Publishing Company Inc., 1993.

Briggs Myers, Isabel and Myers, Peter B. *Gifts Differing.* Palo Alto, California: Davies-Black Publishing, 1995.

Campbell, Joseph. *The Power of Myth.* New York, New York: Bantam Doubleday Dell Publishing Group, Inc., 1988.

Catlette, Bill and Hadden, Richard. *Contented Cows Give Better Milk.* Germantown, Tennessee: Saltillo Press, 2001.

Covey, Steven R. *The Seven Habits of Highly Effective People.* New York, New York: Simon and Schuster, 1989.

Emery, Gary and Campbell, James. *Rapid Relief from Emotional Distress.* New York, New York: Rawson and Associates, 1986.

Fulghum, Robert. *All I Really Need to Know I Learned in Kindergarten.* Toronto, Ontario: Random House of Canada Limited. 1991.

Goleman, Daniel. *Emotional Intelligence.* New York, New York: Bantam Doubleday Dell Publishing Group, Inc., 1997.

Gowing, Marilyn K., Kraft, John D. and Quick, James Campbell. *The New Organizational Reality.* Washington, District of Columbia: American Psychological Association, 1997

Handy, Charles. *The Hungry Spirit.* London, England: Arrow Books, 1998.

Hendricks, Gay and Ludeman, Kate. *The Corporate Mystic.* New York, New York: Bantam Doubleday Dell Publishing Group, Inc., 1997.

Hurley, Kathleen and Dobson, Theodore. *What's My Type?* New York, New York: HarperCollins Publishers, Inc., 1991.

Hyatt, Carole. *Lifetime Employability.* United States: MasterMedia Limited, 1995.

Jarow, Rick. *Creating the Work You Love.* Rochester, Vermont: Destiny Books, 1995.

Lawrence, Gordon. *People Types & Tiger Stripes.* Gainsesville, Florida: Center for Applications of Psychological Type, Inc., 1993.

Maguire, Jack. *The Power of Personal Storytelling.* New York, New York: Penguin Putnam Inc., 1998.

Moore, Thomas. *Care of the Soul.* New York, New York: HarperCollins Publisher, Inc, 1998.

Peck, M. Scott, M.D. *A World Waiting to be Born.* New York, New York: Bantam Books, 1993.

Ruiz, Miguel. *The Four Agreements.* San Rafael, California: Amber-Allen Publishing, Inc., 1997.

Tieger, Paul D. and Barron-Tieger, *Barbara, Do What You Are.* Little, Brown & Company (Canada) Limited, 1995.

Tolle, Eckhart. *The Power of Now.* Novato, California: New World Library, 1999.

Wheatley, Margaret J. *Leadership and the New Science.* San Francisco, California: Berrett-Koehler Publishers, Inc.

Whitmyer, Claude. *Mindfulness and Meaningful Work.* Berkeley, California: Parallax Press, 1994.

Zukav, Gary. *Seat of the Soul.* New York, New York: Simon & Schuster Inc., 1989.

The Conference Board of Canada. *Employability Skills Profile: What are Employers Looking For* brochure identifies *The Critical Skills Required of the Canadian Workforce.* This has been used in *Managing My Development* as a basic framework for developing the Core Attributes Self Assessment *

"The Corporate Council in Education invites and encourages students, parents, teachers, employers, labour, community leaders and governments to use the profile as a framework for dialogue and action,"*